RELIGION AND SPIRITUALITY

ISLAM IN AFRICA AND EUROPE

SELECTED CASE STUDIES

RELIGION AND SPIRITUALITY

Additional books in this series can be found on Nova's website under the Series tab.

Additional e-books in this series can be found on Nova's website under the e-book tab.

RELIGION AND SPIRITUALITY

ISLAM IN AFRICA AND EUROPE

SELECTED CASE STUDIES

NORMAN C. ROTHMAN, PH.D.

New York

Copyright © 2014 by Nova Science Publishers, Inc.

All rights reserved. No part of this book may be reproduced, stored in a retrieval system or transmitted in any form or by any means: electronic, electrostatic, magnetic, tape, mechanical photocopying, recording or otherwise without the written permission of the Publisher.

For permission to use material from this book please contact us:
Telephone 631-231-7269; Fax 631-231-8175
Web Site: http://www.novapublishers.com

NOTICE TO THE READER

The Publisher has taken reasonable care in the preparation of this book, but makes no expressed or implied warranty of any kind and assumes no responsibility for any errors or omissions. No liability is assumed for incidental or consequential damages in connection with or arising out of information contained in this book. The Publisher shall not be liable for any special, consequential, or exemplary damages resulting, in whole or in part, from the readers' use of, or reliance upon, this material. Any parts of this book based on government reports are so indicated and copyright is claimed for those parts to the extent applicable to compilations of such works.

Independent verification should be sought for any data, advice or recommendations contained in this book. In addition, no responsibility is assumed by the publisher for any injury and/or damage to persons or property arising from any methods, products, instructions, ideas or otherwise contained in this publication.

This publication is designed to provide accurate and authoritative information with regard to the subject matter covered herein. It is sold with the clear understanding that the Publisher is not engaged in rendering legal or any other professional services. If legal or any other expert assistance is required, the services of a competent person should be sought. FROM A DECLARATION OF PARTICIPANTS JOINTLY ADOPTED BY A COMMITTEE OF THE AMERICAN BAR ASSOCIATION AND A COMMITTEE OF PUBLISHERS.

Additional color graphics may be available in the e-book version of this book.

Library of Congress Cataloging-in-Publication Data

Islam in Africa and Europe : selected case studies / editor, Norman C. Rothman (Department of History, University of Maryland University College, MD, USA).
     pages cm. -- (Religion and spirituality)
     Includes bibliographical references and index.
     ISBN 978-1-63117-920-4 (hardcover)
     1. Islam--Africa--History. 2. Muslims--Africa. 3. Islam--Europe--History. 4. Muslims--Europe. I. Rothman, Norman C.
     BP64.A1I855 2014
     297.096--dc23
                              2014015859

Published by Nova Science Publishers, Inc. † New York

I dedicate this book to my adoptive and nuclear family.

CONTENTS

Preface		**ix**
Part I: Introduction		**11**
Chapter 1	Background	**13**
Part II: North Africa		**27**
Chapter 2	Algeria	**29**
Chapter 3	Libya	**35**
Part III: West Africa		**41**
Chapter 4	Mali	**43**
Chapter 5	Nigeria	**51**
Part IV: East Africa		**59**
Chapter 6	Somalia	**61**
Chapter 7	Tanzania	**69**
Part V: Caucasus		**77**
Chapter 8	Azerbaijan: Between Asia and Europe	**79**
Chapter 9	Dagestan	**87**
Chapter 10	Chechnya	**93**
Part VI: The Balkans		**99**
Chapter 11	The Albanian World	**101**

Contents

Chapter 12	Bosnia	**109**
Part VII: The Muslim Diaspora in Europe		**117**
Chapter 13	Muslims in France	**121**
Chapter 14	The United Kingdom	**125**
Chapter 15	Germany	**131**
Part VIII: Conclusion		**137**
Endnotes		
Bibliography of Books and Articles		**157**
Glossary		**167**
Author's Contact Information		**177**
Index		**183**

PREFACE

This book is of interest to both the general reader and the student of Islamic, African, and European Affairs. It gives the historical and contemporary state of Islam in selected countries in Africa and Europe. Part one, a general introduction, reviews the arrival and evolution of Islam on the continents of Africa and Europe.

Part II through Part VII concentrates on specific regions. Part II deals with North Africa with case studies on Algeria and Libya. Part III examines West Africa with the focus on Mali and Nigeria. Part IV treats East Africa with studies of Somalia and Nigeria. Part V covers the Caucasus as it is concerned with Azerbaijan, Dagestan, and Chechnya. Part VI concentrates on the Balkan with chapters on the Albanian world and Bosnia respectively. Part VII discusses the Muslim diaspora in Europe through a scrutiny of the role in Islam in France, the United Kingdom (Great Britain), and Germany. Part VIII is devoted to concluding comments. Beyond the citations and references, the book provides a glossary of terms as well as an index.

In addition to the obvious fields of Islamic, African, and European Studies, this inter-disciplinary work is of interest to students of history, government, comparative religion, and general anthropology and sociology with its focus on culture and society. It is the concluding volume of a trilogy that covers Islam on a global basis.

PART I: INTRODUCTION

Chapter 1

BACKGROUND

Islam today competes with Christianity as the most prevalent religion in Africa. It has been an integral part of the continent since its early days. Historically, this association can be viewed as part of a continuum as the connection between the Arabian Peninsula and the continent of Africa predates Islam. The Red Sea between Arabia and Northeast Africa was a corridor for trade and culture. In addition, North Africa and Southwest Asia including the Arabia are linked by the Sinai Peninsula. Moreover, the West African grassland belt between the Sahara belt and the rainforest belt which extends from the Atlantic Ocean to the Red Sea has been a cultural transmission area for ideas and trade. It has also been linked by various routes to North Africa (which became an extension of the Middle East culturally after 700 C.E.) since Paleolithic times. Finally, the Nile River Valley which extends some three thousand miles from the twin origins in Uganda and Ethiopia (the White and Blue Nile) to the Mediterranean Sea has also been a cultural transmission area that binds North Africa and Egypt to East Africa.[1]

Within these overall cultural transmission areas in which influences including Islam have spread are smaller belts. Thus, the Gezira region in North Central Sudan where the Blue and White Niles form the Main Nile and is also part of the horizontal grassland belt has been a particular nodal point. The Mediterranean also links North Africa and Europe and historically been a jumping off point for Islam.[2]

Accordingly, Africa has played a key role in of Islam since the earliest days. Even before the official start of the Islamic calendar (622 C E.), Muhammad advised his followers to flee to Axum, then a flourishing kingdom in Northeast Ethiopia, through its port of Adulis on the Red Sea coast.

Spreading southeast to the Somali coast from the Ethiopian highlands, Islam gradually spread by means of family and lineage connections, trade, and war as well as active missionary work. In the succeeding centuries, the African Red Sea Coast and the Indian Ocean coast witnessed the arrival of Islam by 800.[3]

The major thrust of Islam in Africa in the first centuries after the origin of Islam was in Egypt and the Maghrib (North Africa west of Egypt and the adjoining Cyrenaica region of Northeast Libya), as well as the adjoining areas in the grassland region. Ultimately, as will be shown in the later chapters, the grassland regions were the conduits for the arrival of Islam in the adjoining rainforest region.[4]

Egypt set the pattern for the rest of North Africa. It was conquered in 641 and in part was aided by the Byzantine persecution of its Monophysite (the deity is composed of G-d the father, G-d the son, and the Holy Ghost) now Coptic church. In the eleventh century, permanent Islamic demographic predominance was secured by the migrations of several Arab tribes from the Arabian Peninsula. In Egypt, this is known as the Hillalian invasion after the largest tribe the Bani Hillal.[5]

The conquest of the rest of North Africa or Maghrib ("land of the west" or "land of the sunset" in Arabic) took a bit longer. Technically, the term geographically refers to North Africa west of the Gulf of Sidra in central Libya. Although both the eastern section of the Libyan coast (Cyrenaica) and the western section of the coast (Tripolitania) had been conquered by 643, it took several decades before the rest of the North African littoral was conquered (698-714).[6] It was final accomplished through two factors — the development of an Islamic navy aided by Muslim privateers or corsairs which could attack the coastal cities, and the conversion of the indigenous inhabitants of the interior, the Berbers, who became fervent Muslims. They were an indispensible part of the Muslim conquest of the Iberian Peninsula and parts of France between 711 and 732. By the mid-8th century, the North African coast and its immediate hinterland had become the most Islamized area outside of the original Arabian homeland.

In succeeding centuries, Islam spread further south so that it spread to the desert and converted many nomadic or semi-nomadic Berber tribes. These newly converted Berbers and their descendants formed military brotherhoods which were to dominate much of North Africa between 1000 and 1350.[7] The first of these brotherhoods were the Almoravids who conquered much of Morocco and part of Algeria and then went on to invade the Iberian Peninsula and helped bring about the conversion of many erstwhile Christians to Islam.

They also invaded to the south and helped bring an end to the ancient Ghanaian empire in 1076. They were succeeded by the Almohads who were at their height in the early 1200's. These militant orders secured the dominance of Islam in the Sahara desert and the northern grassland areas (the Sahel) by 1350.[8]

The indigenous Berbers soon adopted many Islamic customs and commingled these customs with their own. They established their own dynasties. The most prominent was the Fatimids — the first prominent dynasty which was Shia, By the mid-10th century, it controlled much of North Africa, and even after the loss of power in the Maghrib by the mid-eleventh century, it ruled Egypt and, at times, Syria and Palestine until the mid-twelfth century. They proclaimed a rival caliphate to the one in Baghdad. They founded Cairo and the most famous Islamic university Al-Azhar. Under their rule, Egypt became both Islamized and Arabized as the Coptic element declined. In fact, although North Africa became predominantly Sunni, it has witnessed a series of schisms. There was support for various form of Shia (the belief that only a lineal descendant of Muhammad can rule and that there should not be any distinction between political and spiritual leadership). The Kharijites held the same beliefs but went further. They maintained that any departure from the exact prescriptions of the Qur'an were grounds for exclusion form the world-wide Muslim legal/political community or umma.[9]

The constant sectarian debates have been a source of conflict in North Africa since 740. Brotherhoods or tariquas of various types have not only been prominent in Algeria, Libya, Morocco, and Tunisia but also in adjacent countries such as Mauritania south of Morocco and Sudan south of Egypt. These orders took various forms. One form which continues even today is of the Sufi variety. Sufism stresses devotional aspects and the mystical link between the practitioner and the Almighty. Sufi followers emphasize the spiritual over the material world. They believe in meditation not political action. By 1000 C.E, they had as elsewhere, produced a series of poets and philosophers in North Africa as well as elsewhere in the Muslim world.[10]

The other form of brotherhoods was militant fraternities. After 1050, the immigration of the Bani Hillal (mostly but not confined to Egypt) but also the Bani Sulaym west of Egypt led to the gradual Arabization of much of North Africa especially on the coast and the interior areas adjacent to the coast. The Berber element gradually retreated to the desert and mountains. By now, they had been converted to Islam. The Berbers used military fortifications (originally used by the Arabs against the Berbers) to promote religious observances. These military-religious fortifications or ribats became staging areas and completed the conversion of the inhabitants in these mountains and deserts to Islam. The orders that devolved from these ribats emphasized a puritanical form of Islam, with a stress on strict adherence to the Qur'an and Sharia law. They are in direct contrast to the mystical monasticism of the Sufi orders. Although the Almoravids (literally men from the ribat) and Almohads are most famous in world history, other orders active in the Maghreb have the Quadariyya (a world-wide order), the Senusiyya (an order based in Cyrenaica and the Fezzan, in central Libya), and the Tijaniyya, a later order active in both North and West Africa.[11]

In contrast to the predominantly military character of the arrival of Islam in North Africa, the arrival of Islam in other parts of Africa came by various routes which will be shortly discussed. West Africa can be divided into two zones. The northern zone which is grassland in the north and a combination of grassland and woodlands in the south lies between the Sahara Desert in the north and the West African rainforest in the south. It encompasses the countries of Senegal, Mauritania, Burkina Faso, Gambia, Mali, Chad, Niger, and Sudan as well as northern sections of Guinea, Liberia, Ivory Coast, Liberia, Sierra Leone, Ghana, Togo, Benin, Nigeria, and Cameroon. The area immediately south of this area and bordered by the Atlantic Ocean is mixed in religious affiliation, but its northern area is dominated by Islam.[12]

Islam came to the northern belt called the Sudanic belt and sometimes the Sahel belt (although that more properly refers to the northern fringe of this area), by direct conquest, trade, and family lineage. The western part of this belt witnessed a series of empires based on trade. The earliest empire, Ghana, fell to Almoravid troops in 1076. Its successor, the Susu Empire, fell to the forces of the Muslim state of Mali in 1235. It in turn, fell to another Islamic Empire, Songhay, in 1494. After defeat by Morocco in 1591, state formation in this area declined especially as its main item of trade, gold specie, was superseded by gold and silver imported from North and South America. Nevertheless, the foundation of Islam had been laid. The most famous of the cities in this area was Timbuktu which became almost as famous for its learning as for its wealth. The celebrated university of Sankore was located here. These states became the areas of dispersal for Islam especially to the South after 1500.[13]

The central and eastern sections of the Sudan gradually converted to Islam after 1000 A.D./C.E. They were often converted by Moslem missionaries as well as by trade. A series of trading routes –the western from Morocco, the central from Algeria, and Tunisia, and the eastern from Tripoli traded goods from North Africa such as salt and cloth in return for goods such as gold, ivory, rhinoceros horn, and occasionally slaves. The main item was the gold available from the Volta River from Wangara and Bouake.[14] The trade somewhat in exaggeration is often called the Silent Trade of the Moors as occasionally the traders from North Africa would leave their goods on the river bank. If the Africans were satisfied, they would leave a rough approximation in gold and other merchandise on the river bank overnight. The central area was dominated by the Kanuri state of Kanem-Bornu which was located before 1500 northeast of Lake Chad and afterwards on the southwest of Lake Chad and became converted to Islam (or at least its ruling dynasty did) by 1100. The Hausa city-states in what is now northern Nigeria also gradually converted to Islam after 1100. Traders from the Sudanic empires (many of Mande origins from Mali) spread Islam especially through trading networks based on kinship.[15] In contrast; the previously Christian states of Dongala and Alwa in eastern Sudan fell to Turkish conquest after 1500. Even in the eastern Sudan, however, there were Muslim states such as Darfur and Wadai in what is today the border between Sudan and Chad.[16]

The initial conversion to Islam had been motivated by the economic benefits to be gained by trade with fellow Muslims in the vast Islamic world. As such the earliest converts had been in the cities and among the upper and merchant classes. However, Islam gradually spread to the rural areas and among the lower classes in West Africa due to the influence of Sufi orders. Sufism stressed folklore over book learning as exemplified by knowledge of the Qur'an and Haditha based on knowledge of Arabic. The less doctrinaire approach made religious ceremonies open to African customs such as dancing and meditation. Syncretism was also encouraged through the visiting of shrines and worship of saints was also compatible with African customs. The overall approach which involved ancestor worship which often had votive power made Islam attractive to many illiterate peasants.[17]

Historically and in contemporary times, Islamic brotherhoods and orders have enjoyed great popularity among the masses. In Senegal and Gambia, for example, the indigenous Murridiyya founded in the 20th century has millions of followers. Another Sufi order, the Tijaniyya, founded at the end of the 18th century is perhaps the most popular order in West Africa especially in the northern part of the Sudanic belt or Sahel in countries such as Mauritania, Mali, and Niger as well as Senegal; and Gambia.[18]

Periodically, there have been waves of Islamic reform which have resulted in revolutions against the established order. Between 1725 and 1860, for instance, a series of Islamic revolts in connection with the Fulani peoples reinforced Muslim performance in Guinea, Senegal, Mali, Niger, and especially in Hausaland (the northern half of Nigeria and adjoining parts of Cameroon). Nigeria is the most populous state in Africa. Today, Nigeria has the fifth largest population of Muslims in the world and has now surpassed Egypt, Iran, and Turkey.[19]

The rainforest areas of West Africa have a greater percentage of Christian and animists but have sizeable Muslim populations in the northern sections often approaching 50% in Ghana, Togo, Benin, Sierra Leone, Liberia, Nigeria, and Cameroon. There is, as will be shown, increasing visibility on the part of orthodox Muslims such as adherents to Salafists aided by organizations such as the World Muslim League and the World Assembly of Muslim Youth and supported financially by Saudi Arabia and other oil-rich Arab Muslim Gulf states. In Nigeria, the Islamist Boko Haram has emerged as a direct threat to the government of Nigeria.[20]

East Africa experienced a more peaceful penetration of Islam along its coast between 750 and 1000 C.E. Presently, the countries of Mauritius, Comoros, Tanzania, Somalia, and Djibouti have Muslim or near Muslim majorities. In the largest populated country in East Africa, Ethiopia, they may constitute a majority. In other countries of East Africa such as Kenya and Mozambique they have significant numbers. They also have a considerable presence in such East Central African countries as Congo and the lake states such as Burundi, Rwanda, and Uganda. Although the coast of Somalia and the adjoining states of Djibouti and Eritrea on the Horn of Africa at the foot of the Red Sea as well as adjacent regions of Ethiopia composed of Somali and Oromo groups were gradually infiltrated by Muslim influences between 750 and 1250, the major source of Islamic influence before 1500 was the Swahili culture.[21]

The Swahili culture extended 2000 miles from present-day Mogadishu in southern Somalia to Cape Delgado in central Mozambique. Although it encompasses only a strip of land of about 12 to 120 miles inland, it also includes the archipelago and islands off the East African coast in the Indian Ocean and included the islands of the Comoros, Zanzibar, and Pemba as well as the northeastern part of Madagascar. In all, it was composed of over four hundred settlements.[22]

Swahili culture was an amalgam of Bantu and Arab with immigrants from the Arabian Peninsula, as well as admixtures from Persia and Muslims from India. The structure of the language was Bantu but with Arab borrowings. The written language was Arabic but by 1500 a Swahili language had emerged which used Arabic letters. As will be shown shortly, Islam was an integral part of the Swahili culture which had emerged by 1000 C.E. The influence of

Background 19

Swahili is so great that today that although relatively small in numbers, it is an official language of Kenya, Tanzania, and Uganda. Because of the trading networks established by the Swahili culture, it is today a second language in a number of countries in East and East Central Africa.[23]

Historically, the Swahili city-states were the middlemen between the interior of Africa and the vast Indian Ocean trading network. They would obtain products from the interior such as gold, ivory, copper, timber, animal skins, rock crystal, and frankincense to sell overseas. In return, products from countries along the littoral of the Indian Ocean and Red Sea such as glass from Egypt, silk from China, textiles from India, and kohl sticks and tea from Persia and Ceylon. Pottery, ceramics, and porcelain were imported from throughout the Indian Ocean. The products imported from abroad were converted into finished products such as textiles into cloth at workshops, and pottery from glazed in local kilns. Goods imported from the interior such as gold, copper, and iron were also converted into finished goods such as nails and knives through smelting, forging and advanced processes such as annealing, oxidation, and open crucibles.[24]

Islamic influence permeated this culture even when much of the Swahili coast fell under Portuguese control between 1506 and 1729.[25] In addition to literacy in Swahili based on Arabic script, literacy in Arabic was considered a sign of culture and upper class. Mosques were the most important buildings in the towns. In some places, they were the dividing line between patricians and commoners as in the Middle East. The mosques exhibited typical Muslim features such as mehrabs, kubilu, and minarets. They naturally faced the Muslim holy cities of Mecca and Medina. The elite wore Muslim ceremonial clothing on special days such as the long white robe, a turban, a sword and dagger, and sandals made of animal hides. Architecture and social space tended to mirror the Islamic world. Not only did the mosques reflect Middle Eastern motifs but the houses of the upper classes reflected the living quarters of the Middle East. They were often multi-storied with a front portico an inner courtyard. They were divided into private and public rooms. The palaces of the local ruler were modeled on Baghdad and Cairo. Upper class males went first to the local elementary or Qur'anic schools and later the madrassas or local schools. A few even went on to Al-Azhar in Cairo. Muslim dietary laws were followed. Some local families even though of Bantu (technically Niger-Congo language family) ancestry even gave themselves myth of origin in terms of Muslim derivation.[26]

Muslims have been involved in Europe since the very early days. Although nowadays one thinks of Muslims in terms of the Balkans and

Caucasus on the fringes of Europe and the recent Muslim immigrant diaspora, the reality is quite different. Sicily was attacked as early as the 7th century and conquered between 827 and 950.[27] During the period of Islamic rule, (which lasted until 1072 when Norman adventurers re-conquered the island) large sections of the population converted to avoid paying the non-believer or jizya tax. The religion maintained itself until the 13th century.[28]

More extensive and lasting were Muslim expeditions into the Iberian Peninsula which led to an occupation which lasted almost eight centuries. They invaded in 711 and occupied most of the peninsula (today occupied by Spain and Portugal). The Muslim conquest was so complete that Al-Andulus as the Muslims termed Iberia at one time occupied all of the peninsula except the northwestern fringe of Asturias, the Basque country, and Navarre — areas which abutted the Pyrenees. The peninsula was reputed to even have a Muslim majority until the Christian kingdoms captured much of Andalusia in 1236 and many Christians reconverted back. The last Muslim kingdom, Granada, fell in 1492. There was a golden age for Muslim states especially in Cordova which formed a third caliphate between the mid 8th[th] and early11[th] century and was famous for its arts and letters. Muslims were forced to convert in 1502. Their conversion was nominal, however, and they were (as Moriscos) permanently expelled between 1609 and 1611.[29]

Muslims also invaded France until stopped by Charles Martel in 732 at the battle of Tours or Poitiers (the exact site is still being debated). Nonetheless, they were a major presence in France between 719 and 759. In fact, southwestern France called Septimania was an administrative section of Al-Andalus. Even after 759, they held sections of France between France and Switzerland until 950. Although their footprint is small in France, the Muslim heritage is more evident in the language and the architecture as well as the genetics of Spain.[30]

During the first millennium, there were continued Muslim incursions in Europe. In fact, if Barbary pirates are included, these raids lasted until the early 19th century. Therefore, parts of southern Italy fell under Muslim control between 850 and 1000 C.E. They even sacked Rome in 861 and Pisa in 1034.[31] Muslims also controlled sections of Sardinia and Corsica until 1500. They were a threat to the western Mediterranean and such outposts as Malta until the battle of Lepanto in 1571.[32]

Even in later centuries, Muslim pirates from coastal parts of Morocco, Algeria, Tunisia, and Tripoli (the Barbary pirates) raided Christian ships and coasts of Spain, Portugal, Italy, France, England, Ireland, Scotland, the

Netherlands, the Azores, and Iceland. These raids were especially virulent between the 16th and 19th centuries.[33]

Islam spread into eastern and southern Europe through conquest. Even before this time, however, Vikings from Scandinavia had traded with Muslims through the extensive river system in what is now Russia to the Black and Caspian Seas –the fabled Western and Eastern passages to the Middle East. States located in the Caucasus on the edge of Europe also traded with the Islamic world.

More often particularly after 1000, the arrival of Muslims came with military conquest. Groups of Turkic–speaking invaders (later called Tatars) under Mongol command began to convert to Islam. One of the first Turkic groups to convert was the Bulgars of the Volta who retain their religion even today. After the conquest of much of what is today Russia and Ukraine which fell under Mongol/Tatar control by Genghis Khan and his successors in the early 13th century, the conversion of the ruling Mongol/Tatars left pockets of Muslims along the Volga River and the Black Sea.[34]

Even after the expansion of Russia/Muscovy in the 16th century, the conquest of Kazan and Astrakhan at both ends of the Volga River and at the entry of the Urals — the dividing line between Asia and Europe left many Muslims intact albeit under Russian rule mostly Tatars and Bashkirs. Afterward, the Khanate of Crimea, composed of Tatars, remained independent until 1783. Although the Tatars of Crimea were deported to Central Asia as an enemy group during WWII along with the Balkars, Chechens, Ingush, and other Caucasus Muslim groups (before being allowed to return in the late fifties and sixties), they remained practicing Muslims during and after the Soviet period.[35]

As the Caucasus were the last part of the European Russian to be annexed, large sections of Muslims remain, The peoples of the North Caucasus had gradually become converted to Islam between the 8th and 18th centuries. Today, Chechens, Ingush, and various Dagestan groups as well as smaller groups scattered through the Caucasus have continued to practice Islam (see the chapters on Chechnya and Dagestan).[36]

The North Caucasian peoples survived the Soviet period with their Islamic beliefs intact as did the people of Azerbaijan which had the largest single group of Muslims in the former Soviet Union. Azerbaijan is located in the southern Caucasus and borders the Caspian Sea — the southern border between Europe and Asia. It came into contact with Islam as early as 650 when Arabs brought Islam to the country. When it was occupied by Azeri Turks, it retained Islam. In 1501, it came under Persian rule and adopted Shia

Islam. In 1828, Persia gave up the northern part of the country to Russia and the southern part remained under Persian control — a division which remains today. Russian Azerbaijan retained its Muslim faith under Soviet rule. Today, as an independent country it is about 60% Shia mostly in the south and 40% Sunni in the north. There is a strong irredentist movement which seeks union with the 11/12 million Azeri's currently under Iranian (formerly Persian) rule.[37]

The other area of historical concentration of European Muslims is in the Balkans in Southeast Europe. This is the heritage of the Ottoman Empire –a Turkic-dominated state which ruled much of the Middle East and North Africa as well as Southeast Europe for over 5 centuries from the late 1300's to WWI. It conquered Constantinople in 1453, and the Turks ruled what is today Greece, Bulgaria, Albania, Serbia, Romania, Macedonia, Bosnia, and parts of Hungary and Moldova. After their highpoint at the siege of Vienna in 1683, the Ottoman Turks were pushed back until it reached its present borders after WWI. It now consists of eastern Thrace and Istanbul (the former Constantinople) approximately 11,000 square miles since 1923-24 when the current republic was proclaimed.[38] Since this time, many Muslims from Bulgaria and Romania have migrated to Turkey proper and there was an exchange of populations with Greece in 1924. Afterward, there were further migrations of Illyrians (Albanians also called Chams) from Epirus in northwest Greece to Turkey. The only change in the Muslim population under Muslim rule has been in northern Cyprus. In 1973, Turkey invaded the island and set up a rump state for the 20% which was Muslim but now occupies nearly 40% of the area.[39]

The areas of Bosnia (and Herzegovina – the southern fourth of Bosnia) as well as the Albanian population in Albania proper in addition to adjoining Kosovo, Macedonia, the Preservo valley in Serbia, the Sanjak of Novi Pazar between Serbia and Montenegro, and eastern Montenegro have seen the largest Muslim imprint. The Turks accomplished this situation largely through conversion. Conversion to Islam meant freedom from the jizya or non-believer tax. Moreover conversion opened opportunity for rise through the Ottoman bureaucracy or through the military. In this last case, Christian boys would be recruited for the Turkish military or janissary corps. Promotion could come through conversion as it would through civil employment. The long period of control aided in this process.[40]

Special circumstances aided in the conversion in some cases. In Bosnia where Ottoman rule lasted from 1480 to 1878, the Turks took advantage of rivalries among Christians. First, there was a schismatic religious sect (also active in Bulgaria), the Bogomils. There was a separate Bosnian Church. These two factions were persecuted by Rome. Bosnia was caught in the rivalry between Rome and the Byzantine Empire so that there was bad blood between their respective Roman Catholic and Orthodox factions. As a consequence, the conversion rate had reached 40% of the population by the end of the 16th century.[41]

Among Albanians, the intramural rivalry between the northern Roman Catholic clans and southern Orthodox clans also provided an opening for the Ottomans who remained in Albania until 1913. By playing rival groups off against each other, mass conversion at between 80 to 90% Muslim supremacy was achieved within a century.[42]

Demographic trends have also affected neighboring areas. As the Albanian population increased, Albanians emigrated and joined other Albanian-speaking populations. They brought their religion with them. With Ottoman encouragement to increase a loyal population, the Muslim percentage increased in all Albanian populated areas. In Kosovo, the Albanian population increased at the expense of the Serbs so that today after the NATO campaign of 1999 and the Kosovo declaration of independence in 2010, the majority of people are Albanian (90%) and the majority of these are Muslims.[43]

Other Albanian population centers reflect these tendencies. It is projected by some that Albanians as an ethnic group may constitute a majority in Macedonia by 2050. Muslims constitute a plurality here too although there is a Christian component (Mother Teresa was born here of Albanian heritage). There is the same relative increase in the other Albanian centers in Montenegro, the Sanjak, and Preservo. Due to the density of population and economic factors, however, a large number of Albanians have emigrated. There are also a number of Slavic Muslims (apart from Bosnians) in the Balkans.[44]

The population of Muslims in Western Europe has dramatically increased since WWII. Its original impetus was due to a number of factors — aging population pyramids in Europe as well as labor shortages caused by the war, and perception of opportunity by immigrant groups. The push factors for immigrants including Muslims from the Middle East, North Africa, and South Asia encompassed political unrest and political deprivation. In recent years, it is estimated that the perhaps 85% of the population increase is due to immigration.[45]

The causes and configuration of Muslim immigration vary from country to country. In Germany, the Muslim population is mostly Turkish with some Palestinians. It had its origins in the need of what was then West Germany for guest workers due to labor shortages caused by losses during WWII. France, not quite facing the same population needs, nonetheless, became a home to many Muslim immigrants because of the Algerian War (1954-1962) and the end of the French colonial empire in North Africa. Today, because of relative prosperity and geographical proximity via the Mediterranean, Muslim refugees from North Africa and the Middle East go to Italy, Spain, and Portugal. Their membership in the European Union means that arrivals can go elsewhere in Europe.[46]

A number of European countries receive Muslim migrants as a legacy of former empires. The Netherlands, for example, receives Muslims (and Christians) from its former colony of the Dutch East Indies (Indonesia). As was indicated before, France receives migrants from its North African colonies (not only Algeria but also Morocco and Tunisia). To some extent, it also receives innigration from former West African and Central African colonies which includes a percentage of Muslims. It also receives immigrants from its former protectorates of Lebanon and Syria. The United Kingdom receives many immigrants from Pakistan and India (which has a large Muslim population) as well as former African colonies with their share of Muslims. Even Belgium receives immigrants from its former colony of Congo (a good percentage of which are Muslim).[47]

Other countries receive immigrants including Muslims because of a tradition as a refuge for persecuted groups. The Scandinavian countries of Denmark, Norway, and Sweden have provided a haven for Kurds, Somali, and Bosnian Muslims. Switzerland has done the same. Austria has provided a refuge for Muslim emigrants from the Balkans and Middle East.[48]

There are other Muslim communities that are not often counted. For example, there are communities of Turkish and Slavic Muslims in Bulgaria, Moldova, Montenegro, and Serbia. A number of young European has been attracted to certain aspects of Islam. Sufism with its emphasis on meditation and devotion has caused a number of conversions. There are increasing unions between Christians and Muslims with offspring often being raised as Muslims. As Muslims are the largest single group of migrants and have a higher birth rate, the percentage of Muslims is increasing.[49]

The increasing number of Muslims coupled with ancient sectarian animosities has caused a great number of conflicts in recent decades especially within the border region of the Caucasus. Predominantly Orthodox Georgia has had struggles with the Abkhazia and South Ossetia which seceded with Russian assistance. The Armenian Christian enclave of Nagorno-Karabakh, placed within predominantly Muslim Azerbaijan when Stalin engaged in his favorite game of mix and match when drawing boundaries, was a source of conflict between the two countries after the breakup of the Soviet Union. Occupied by Armenia, its embittered Muslim refugees have added to anti-Armenian protests within Azerbaijan. The Caucasus has also seen ongoing Islamic resistance to Russia (see chapters on Chechnya and Dagestan). Within Western Europe, there has also been sectarian related conflict. In recent years especially in 2005, there were riots in the suburbs of Paris which spread to other urban areas of France by Muslim youth who rioted against feels of discrimination and chronic unemployment, In the United Kingdom, there were extremist outbreaks in London, Hull, and Sheffield tied to radical imams. In return, there have been anti-Muslim protests and riots in Stockholm, Sweden and Sofia, Bulgaria.[50]

There are other issues which have roiled relations between Muslims and other groups in the last two decades. These have included the prohibition of Islamic garb especially headscarfs in French schools, the introduction of Sharia in certain parts of Muslim areas in the United Kingdom, and the issue of citizenship in Germany which was previously based on blood and descent for long-time residents. Several countries have threatened deportation.[51]

On the other side, the prospect of creeping Islamization has agitated young people who are more secular in predominantly Muslim areas such as Azerbaijan, Chechnya, and Turkey especially in schools. The recent anti-government protests in Istanbul were primarily against the perceived policies of the Erdogan government. Collectively, his actions in recent years have been interpreted as blows against Turkey's nearly century-old secularization policy.[52]

The overall issue in Europe in regard to Islam has become one of accommodation verses assimilation. How does reconcile the needs of Muslims with the perceived interests of civil society? Is conflict inevitable? Are the unfortunate situations of the Greek-Turkish conflict over Cyprus, the Armenian-Azeri conflict over Nagorno-Karabakh, the dispute of Georgia with Abkhazia and South Ossetia, the struggle of Albanian with Serb in Kosovo, the Islamic struggles in the Caucasus especially in Chechnya and Dagestan against Russia, and three sided sectarian violence in Bosnia, the wave of the future?

We, in the United States, have a European heritage, but the country historically and once again is a country of global immigration so that accommodation has been part of the fabric of this nation since the beginning including to a greater or lesser degree Muslims from overseas. In contrast, Europe traditionally has been a region of emigration. It has (at least in Europe) been composed of nation-states which are ethnically and religiously and culturally homogeneous. The arrival of groups of people with new cultures (predominantly Muslim) has not been a part of its national mission. It therefore is in search of a paradigm in order to deal with an unprecedented situation.

Islam in both Africa and Europe can be a unifying or disruptive force. It has been both in the past. The challenge in the future for both civil society in both Africa and Europe is to devise a framework wherein Islam can be part of a multi-faceted modern society.

PART II: NORTH AFRICA

Chapter 2

ALGERIA

Typical of North Africa, over 98% of its 40 million people is Muslim in Algeria. The advent of Islam has been pervasive through the region –Libya, Tunisia, Algeria, and Morocco. It has affected every social institution — the military, education, politics, the economy, etc. in one degree or another.[1]

The process has been length and complicated. Because North Africa occupied the southern shore of the Mediterranean west of Egypt, it was considered strategically important by the early rulers in Islam. Libya or its coastal regions were conquered early Cyrenaica in 641 and Tripolitania in 643. However, the true conquest of the Maghrib (North Africa west of the Gulf of Sidra in central Libya) did not begin until 670 when the Muslims had developed a navy with which they could besiege the most Christian settlements on the coast. By 711 coastal North Africa with the adjacent plains had been conquered aided by the pastoral semi-nomadic Berbers of the plains had been conquered, The Arab conquerors established their headquarters at Qayrawan south of Tunis. Although the Berbers had aided in the conquest of Iberia, by 740, they were in revolt. After this period, the essential unity of North Africa was often broken. Some of the states were Shia while others were Kharijite. The vast interior of Algeria composed of the Khabalye mountains and the Sahara desert did not fully become Islamized until after 1000.[2]

For a while, a locally supported dynasty, the Fatimids, took control of much of Algeria as well as other parts of North Africa and Egypt. After the decline of this Shiite dynasty (which proclaimed a second caliphate in Cairo) by the late 11th century, Algeria began an area of conflict between reviving Sunni orthodox groups and the Shia/Kharijite groups.[3] It was led by two Berber movements — the Almoravids and then the Almohads who led a Sunni revival movement and occupied Muslim Iberia and North Africa including much of Algeria.[4] After the decline of the latter group in the mid-thirteenth century, central authority began to break down. Local rulers arose which were subservient to dynasties from Morocco or Tunisia. The coastal cities were dominated by merchants.[5] Often European powers from the Normans as early as the 11th century to the Spaniards who ruled Oran and occasionally Constantine until 1797 were involved in politics.[6] Bedouin Arab groups which also arrived by 1100 added to this changing mosaic.[7]

Between 1500 and 1815, Algeria was influenced by pirates and privateers as well as the Ottoman Empire. With their cohorts from Tunis, Tripoli, and Morocco, the Barbary pirates as they were called plundered the Mediterranean and Europe.[8] Internally, the Ottoman Empire took over much of North Africa with the exception of Morocco. Until 1587, military representatives governed with the title of Pasha. The country was administered by Janissaries from Turkey with Turkish as the language of administration. Over the course of time, control loosened so that by 1671, locally appointed rulers with the title of Dey or Bey governed the major cities with the surrounding countryside. There really was no central authority (even though Algiers was the nominal seat of administration) as a number of cities had their rulers or deys. In reality, under the nominal sovereignty of the Ottoman Empire, the local aristocracy controlled much of the countryside.[9]

During this period, a two-fold religious situation (which persists to some extent today) developed. The cities followed the traditional Sunni Orthodox practice in terms of following the Qur'an and being guided by religious scholars such as the ulama. The practice in the countryside was quite different. Outside of the cities with their emphasis on mosques and schools, many people found inspiration from wandering holy men or marabouts. These individuals were believed to possess spiritual grace or Baraka. In rural areas, they would offer spiritual guidance and even mediate financial or political disputes. Similar to Sufi practice, they often attained a type of sainthood after death so that their tombs became shrines to which practitioners made pilgrimages. They were an object of veneration. Often they became the "de facto" head of autonomous republics which dotted the countryside in the vast Algerian hinterland. To keep the keep the peace and avoid unrest, the authorities would bestow financial and political benefits on these marabout leaders of these republics. The followers of these holy men would form brotherhoods. The leaders of these brotherhoods would be marabouts or would be called shayks. These leaders who could be Arabic or Berber in origin would

Algeria 31

become politically involved and lead the resistance during the colonial period and afterwards.[10]

THE COLONIAL AND NATIONAL PERIOD

In 1830, under the excuse of an insult to the French Consul, the French occupied Algiers. However, occupying Algiers was a far cry from occupying such a vast country which was nearly four times the size of France. It was not until the early eighteen seventies that resistance was overcome in the far south (the nomadic Berbers/Tuaregs organized in the Sahara Desert as two Bedouin confederations — the Sanhaja and Zenata — were the last to surrender) or actually it was more a matter of occupying space as these groups of pastorals do not recognize borders drawn on a map and wander back and forth into various countries (Algeria, Morocco, Mauritania, the former Spanish Sahara, Mali, Niger, Libya, and Chad). The immediate resistance was led by the leader of a Muslim order, Abd-al Quadir. Taking up arms in the mid eighteen thirties, he was so successful that between 1839 and 1843, he had established a Muslim-centered government which controlled two-thirds of the country. As such, he was a direct threat to the French position. Initially, he was able to rally popular support as it was fairly obvious that the French intended to make Algeria a settler country for French and other Europeans who would bring their religion with them. (In fact, at their height, in the mid twentieth century), European settlers or colons constituted approximately two million out of perhaps 10 million or 20% of the population (almost all of them left after Independence in 1962). Abd-al Quadir with popular support coupled with military talent was able to defeat French arms repeatedly between 1839 and 1843. At length, through sheer numbers –the French deployed up to 180,000 in the field and modern weaponry which their factories could replace, he was eventually worn down. He surrendered in 1845. After a period of imprisonment, he relocated to Damascus where he engaged in humanitarian activities. Today, he is recognized as the first hero of Algerian independence.[11]

Although opposition to French colonial rule had been centered upon Muslim authorities in the cities and countryside through much of the nineteenth century, anti-French activity became more secular especially after WWI. This was partly due to the attitude of the French left and Socialists (who were also anti-clerical) who opposed the French colonial empire. It was also due to the education that many newly-emerging leaders had received. They had been educated either in Algeria or France itself in modern French high schools and colleges where they had received a western education. Even though many new leaders of the nationalist groups became socialist, they received support from Muslim authorities even Muslim scholars such as the ulama during the nationalist struggle particularly during the Algerian War of Independence which took so many lives lives during the years 1954-62. At this time, the guerrilla forces, the National Liberation Front (FLN) catered to Muslim groups at least rhetorically although the leadership was secularist and socialist. It looked at Islam as useful for political mobilization. It even threw a few bones to religious forces such as the Family Status Code which recognized Sharia in domestic disputes. As Independence had also led to the departure of European colonist and their western non-Islamic groups, at first Muslim groups were satisfied.[12]

Gradually dissatisfaction grew. In in the early decades, Muslim opposition was moderate. The Al-Quijan or Values party pressed for Islamic education under the banner of cultural integrity. The Ir-Irshal, another Islamic movement also supported this goal along with socio-economic rather than political issues. These movements stressed human rights, family law, and economic equity. They were concerned with overall cultural integrity which fit in the nationalist government goals of an Algerian identity.[13]

However, by the nineteen eighties, it was apparent that the government attitude that Islam was useful for political mobilization but not government began to cause opposition among Muslims. This was reinforced by the economic doldrums which set in the nineteen eighties with the collapse of oil prices which had supported the Algerian economy during the first two decades. Muslim critics felt that that the FLN had departed from its original declaration in 1954 that an independent state would be based on Islamic principles. It had become increasingly apparent that the state was being run on secular and socialist principles. In October 1988, riots broke out in Algeria's urban centers and were brutally suppressed. Ultimately, a new radical and modernist organization, the Islamic Salvation Army (FIS) was formed to replace the monopoly of the FLN.[14]

The new organization had both moderate and radical wings. By appealing to the struggling middle class of small merchants, the moderate section also appealed to the somewhat secular civil servants as well as disgruntled college graduates who were jobless, they surprised the country by winning almost half of the legislative seats in parliamentary elections in December 1991. The government and especially the military reacted by cancelling further rounds in the election. Thereafter, the country was polarized between the military controlled government and the Islamic influenced opposition.[15]

Since this action in early 1992, elections have been held under somewhat dubious circumstances. Muslims have felt that they have been unfairly excluded from power. As a consequence, militant radicals departed from the FIS to organize the Armed Islamic Group (GIA). Whereas the FIS sought political power through elections, the GIA believed in jihad to achieve power. Civil war ensued which cost over 150,000 lives.[16]

After 1999, an agreement was reached between the government and the FIS which rejected "dictatorship" and "affirmed individual and collective liberties such as race, sex, religion, and language." After the military denounced the accord, the amnesty was aborted.[17]

Since that time, the current president, Bouteflika, has promoted the end of violence. In 2011, the protests that occurred in other Arab countries were only a on a smaller scale. A number of factors have contributed to a lessening of sectarian violence. The president did ease the military back to the barracks although he and his party have retained absolute power with a rubber stamp parliament. Nonetheless, violence has diminished particularly after a 2005 referendum which granted a second amnesty to armed militants. Moreover, with an improving economy through the discovery of new gas and oil deposits, the government has been able to get away with its unfilled promise of constitutional change. This unfulfilled promise along with continued state control over many enterprises has led to a large exodus of many people overseas especially France to seek better lives — a development that the government has not discouraged as it provides a release for dissatisfied citizens especially educated unemployed young people.[18]

The past 15 years have seen the decline of "official" Islamists. In spite of the 1999 and 2005 accords, the FIS and its militant wing, the Islamic Salvation Army are not allowed officially to contest elections. However, front organizations such as the Movement of the Society for Peace and the Movement for National Reform have been able to vote for the rather powerless parliament.[19]

There have been a succession of armed militant Islamic groups which have bedeviled Algeria and neighboring countries in North and Northwest Africa, The GIA gave way to the Salafist Group for Peace and Contentment (GPSC). At its height, the GSPC had 5 to 7,000 soldiers in the field.[20] After the 2005 accord, the GSPC, in turn, gave way to Al-Qaeda in the Maghreb (AQIM) which announced its allegiance to Bin Laden. It also had branches in Tunisia and Mali. It has declined somewhat as other groups have broken off from it. One of its offshoots, the Signed in Blood battalion has become prominent in hostage taking and terrorist acts.[21] This latter organization was formed in October 2012 and as early as January 2013 it attacked the Armenas gas plant in Southeast Algeria which resulted in great loss of life. In connection with other terrorist groups, it attacked government troops in Niger in May 2013.[22]

Algerian related groups routinely cross borders to hook up with other affiliated militant groups. Another offshoot of AQIM, the Movement for Monotheism and Jihad in West Africa (MUJAO) joined two Tuareg radical Islamic groups in seizing much of north Mali between 2012 and 2013 including the historical town of Gao, the birthplace of the Malian Empire, and the ancient town of Timbuktu — fabled in Medieval times for both its wealth and Islamic learning. Although expelled by both French troops and a force from the African Union, it caused much damage to historical monuments. It also kidnapped several Algerian diplomats in Mali in 2012.[23] This group and other militant groups composed mostly of traditional nomadic Bedouin Tuareg and Jihadist Arabs travel constantly between Algeria and the adjacent countries of Mali, Niger, and Mauritania. MUJAO and its offshoots are active in northern Niger, western Libya, and southeastern Algeria. Citizens of Algeria, Libya, and Mali have the largest contingents. MUJAO's largest offshoot, the Islamic Sahara Movement for Justice, is particularly active and Algerians officials have been special targets.[24]

The activities of these groups, dangerous as they are, are not a continuation of the civil conflict of the 1990's. The Islamic radical groups of that time were mostly homegrown. These groups are transnational bound by Islamic radicalism. However, they feed on the same cause — discontent with the status quo in Algeria. As long as the Algerian government operates in a semi-dictatorial manner and is still seen as promoting a secular and socialist agenda, these militant groups will attract support. An agreement such the abortive accord of 1999, the Rome accord, between moderate Islamic groups such as the civilian branch of the FIS and other moderate Islamic groups which support civil liberties and some degree of pluralism and moderate elements of the FLN and other secular forces would be a useful step to alleviating the present situation in Algeria as would the religious brotherhoods such as the Quadiriyya and the Tijaniyya which still have a presence in the country.[25]

Chapter 3

LIBYA

Libya exemplifies the role of religion in the promotion of national identity. Historically, its three constituent parts — Cyrenaica, Tripolitania, Fezzan, have followed different paths. In the east, Cyrenaica's coast was settled by Greeks who founded a series of settlements including Benghazi and Derna (the historical seat of radical Islam) in the 4th century B.C.E. For periods afterward, it was connected to Egypt such as during the Ptolemaic period. It was successively placed under Roman and Byzantine rule before the Muslim conquest in 641-43.[1]

In contrast, Tripolitania has always been grouped with its western Maghrib neighbors in western North Africa especially its immediate neighbor of Tunisia. This is a matter of both geography and history. As has been indicated early, North Africa west of the Gulf of Sidra in central Libya is considered part of the Maghrib or "west or land of the setting sun" in Arabic. Along with Carthage, Tripoli and other cities of Tripolitania were first settled by Phoenicians in the 6th century B.C.E. Afterward, it fell under the control of the Roman and Byzantine Empire before the advent of Islam in the mid7[th] century. During this period, the interior of Tripolitania along with Central Libya, the Fezzan, was under the sovereignty of indigenous Berber kingdoms such as the Garamantes and Numidians. Even after Arab Muslim conquest and the migration of the Banu Hillal and Sulayam in the 11th centuries, there were (and are) Berbers in the mountain and desert areas.[2]

As was the case with the rest of the Maghrib, after 750, Tripolitania paid obeisance to the Caliph of Baghdad and then the Fatimids of Cairo, but was often ruled by local dynasties who derived from local governors especially after the 13th century. In the 12th and 13th century, it followed its western neighbors and fell under Almoravid and Almohad influence. For a brief period, it was even under Aragonese/Catalans and Knights of St. John control (mostly on the coast between 1350 and 1551). Afterward, the Ottomans directly ruled Cyrenaica and Tripolitania (and Fezzan in between). During this period, Tripoli also prospered from the Trans-Saharan trade which went from Kanem-Bornu to Tripoli and traded gold for salt and other products. In 1711, the Karamanli dynasty took over both Tripoli and Cyrenaica as representatives of the Ottoman Empire and ruled until 1833.[3]

Tripoli, under the Karamanli, was one of the Barbary States and engaged in piracy. The war with the Barbary State of Tripoli which involved an attack on Derna in Cyrenaica is an important episode in American and marine history (not to mention the marine anthem) in 1801-5 which helped to end the practice including the paying of ransom.[4] After 1835, with the breakdown of order, the Karamanli were replaced by direct Ottoman Turkish rule. In 1911, Italy which had been disappointed by the French seizure of Tunisia, took advantage of a Turkey weakened by war in the Balkans to seize Tripoli and Cyrenaica. In 1912, it united Tripolitania, Cyrenaica, and the sparsely populated desert and semi-desert area in between, the Fezzan, to form Libya. Although Tripoli has been the capital of united Libya since then, it has experienced disputes with other regional Tripolitania cities such as Misrata and Zintan since the fall of Khadaffi in 2011.[5]

Fezzan itself the semi-nomadic area between Cyrenaica and Tripolitania had the same history as the rest of the country. It was conquered by Muslim armies around 665 CE and was ruled by local dynasties but was not finally subdued until 1842 and was part of independent Libya in 1951. Its population is composed of both sedentary as well as nomadic Arabs and Berbers as well as a few Africans in the extreme south.[6] The Bedouin groups such as the Tuaregs and Toubous have had internecine quarrels over land and the scarce water oases. Many Fezannis really do not recognize political boundaries which were drawn up in European chanceries only in the 20th century. The nomadic groups take their flocks across borders in countries such as Libya, Chad, Mali, Niger, and Algeria. Their sense of identity is often defined by their clan or ethnic group/tribe before the country in which they reside.[7]

ISLAM IN LIBYA

In terms of religion, Fezzan as well as Cyrenaica became the original Sanussiyya order that not only spread throughout Libya but via the Bedouin spread southward into Chad and Niger. The dynasty and its leaders were at the center of resistance to Italian colonialism. A Sanussiyya leader, Omar Al-Mukhtiar, known as the "Lion of the Desert" successfully resisted the Italians for two decades. The head of the Order (Sufi) became the ruler of Libya when it became independent in 1951 and remained in power until 1969.[8]

Islam in Libya tends to reflect the environment. In the cities and along the coast observance is orthodox with strict adherence to the Qur'an and a reverence for Sharia law. The Berbers of the mountains and the Berbers and Arabs (the descendants of the Bani Sulaym) have tended to form religious brotherhoods or tarikas.[9] Many of these brotherhoods such as most prominently the Sanussiyya furnished fighters for Islam.[10]

There are a number of characteristics of these brotherhoods (similar to those covered in Algeria and to North Africa as a whole). First, these predominantly Berber and Sufi brotherhoods although advocating a strict following of sacred texts stress the personal relationship between the practitioner and the supreme deities. As Berbers, whether Taureg or Toubous, they do or have incorporated pre-Islamic syncretic beliefs (as opposed to the legalistic intellectual Sunni version practiced in the Arab influenced coast especially in Cyrenaican cities such as Benghazi and Derna). Theirs is a popular or folk Islam which emphasizes the beliefs and personal experience of the average person as opposed to the importance of the scholar class or ulama.[11]

Accordingly, folk Islam in Libya incorporates such traditional beliefs as rituals and the use of talisman for good fortune as well as the veneration of local saints (jinns) and religious pilgrimages to their tombs. All of these practices are anathema to the ultra-orthodox. However, they do incorporate indigenous traditions.[12]

The worship of saints is especially prominent in rural and Berber areas. The religious veneration includes the concept of religious charisma which is the belief in special spiritual power in given human beings. This power or baraka which has been discussed previously combines personal blessedness with the aforementioned spiritual power. If follows then that after death these human beings are worthy of worship as saints and the subsequent visits to their tombs. In life, they gather followers so that these mystical teachers and the followers form a group or zawiya.[13]

The eastern trans-Sahara trade route lay between Tripoli and Kanem-Bornu in the Lake Chad region wherein religious interchange flowed both ways. The capital of Kanem-Bornu after 1500 was Birni Gazargana. This city became a noted center of Islamic learning so that Islamic ideas passed along this cultural transmission route as well as gold, ivory, and slaves.[14]

The Sufi-centered orders have formed a mechanism for state formation and national identity. Even before the Sanuisiyya took root in 19th century Libya, the world- wide order, the Quadiriyya was active in the country. This and other orders were composed of local lodges or zawiyas. They in turn formed networks throughout Tripolitania, Cyrenaica, and Fezzan.[15]

The Sanusiyya followed in these steps from its foundation in the city of Bayda in Cyrenaica which bordered Fezzan in 1841. The series of religious and educational centers it started formed centers of resistance against Italian colonialism and was a precursor to the struggle of Omar Al-Muktiar. Although its property was damaged during this struggle and WWII in which Libya was a major theater during the North African campaign, it retained its high prestige in the country.[16]

The status of the order remained so high that its presence persuaded the victorious Allies and the United Nations to go ahead with a united independent Libya as a viable country after WWII. The grandson of the founder of the order, Idris al-Senussi, was thereupon selected as the first head of state after serving as Emir of Cyrenaica for two years. The order was therefore considered an essential component of a Libyan state.[17]

After his overthrow by Kaddafi in 1969, against some expectations, Islam did not experience a setback. On the contrary, there was a revival of orthodox Islam as opposed to the Sufi-oriented syncretic Islam advocated by the Sanuisiyya. Although Khaddafi was considered a socialist and revolutionary, he was or professed to be a devout Muslim. Accordingly, he was initially supported by organized Islam. Unlike the Sufi version which stressed ideals and feeling, Kaddafi advocated a return to fundamentalism and the following of the strictures of the Qur'an as an alternate to the impurities introduced from Europe.[18]

Therefore, the teachings of the Qur'an were to serve as a moral guide. Kaddafi went even further. He published a tract, the Green Book, which he termed a modern adaptation of the Qur'an. It was to be universally followed.[19]

His book was accompanied by acts in the 1970's. All bars, nightclubs, and "provocative" entertainment were closed. The use of the Muslim calendar was made mandatory. In November 1973, a legal code was issued that confirmed to the Sharia. In 1977, it was decreed that all future legal enactments were to conform to the Sharia. This code specifically listed penalties mentioned in religious scriptures. Armed robbery was to be punished by amputation of hand and foot (although never executed), Another official act prescribed the flogging of individuals for breaking the fast of Ramadan. Eighty lashes were to be administered for both parties for fornication.[20]

Even though official Islam had supported Kaddafi in the 1970's, they became disenchanted during the 1980's. He began to attack the religious establishment of the ulama, imams, and jurists. He started to alter his earlier views and saw himself as a refiner of religion. As such, he questioned both the Hadith and Sunna. Even the Sharia, he maintained, only governed religious affairs. He even called for the revisions of the Muslim calendar. Internationally, he took as somewhat different tack, He saw Libya as a teacher of the Islamic world. He supported Islam overseas to the point of setting up a Jihad Fund to support the Palestinians. He financed Islamic centers in Vienna and Bangkok through the Islamic Mission Society. He organized the Islamic Call Society in order to propagate Islam abroad.[21]

Ironically, Kaddafi's open support of Islamic causes abroad caused him to oppose the Muslim Brotherhood inside Libya. He objected to what he felt were their subversive and clandestine methods. His persecution actually assisted the Muslim Brotherhood in attaining popularity throughout the country. It was especially strong in the eastern cities of Bayda, Benghazi, and Derna.[22]

Since Kaddafi's overthrow in 2011, Muslim fundamentalist groups have seen a revival especially in the eastern cities. Nevertheless, they are not quite as strong in Tripoli and other western cities. Because, the west is somewhat more populous, the less sectarian National Forces Party received more than two/thirds of the vote in what was considered a setback for the more fundamentalist parties in 2012 for a two year term. However, since the country is currently in near-chaos, this is an expression of sentiment rather than power. Armed militias including Islamic militants centered in the East hold sway in a number of areas.[23]

On the ground, the Ansar-al-Sharia is the most powerful of the armed Islamic militias. It has units in a number of countries especially Tunisia and Libya. In Libya, it has a number of brigades. They are so open about their operations and activities that when they recently held a meeting in Benghazi more than 1,000 members and sympathizers attended. They are believed to be behind several terrorist attacks in 2012 and 2013. The most infamous of these attacks attributed to Ansar-al-Sharia was the attack on the United States Consulate on September 11, 2012 in which the Ambassador to Libya and three other Americans lost their lives. The suspected mastermind of the attack, Mohammed al-Zawahi, still appears in public. His colleague, Sufan-bin-Qamin, the head of Ansar-al-Sharia in Derna, the traditional headquarters of

Islamism in Libya, has also been linked to the attack. He is a former detainee in Guantanamo. The group along with other militant Islamist organizations has a presence in social media outlets such as Facebook and YouTube. These radical groups have their own blog and websites.[24]

Nowadays, many radical and militant groups have a two-prong strategy which Ansar-al-Sharia has been careful to follow. Following the blueprint of the Muslim Brotherhood in Egypt, Hizbollah in Lebanon, and, to some extent, the IRA in Northern Ireland, it has two faces. It has a public aspect in which it engages in social welfare tasks such as street cleaning and repair, aid to the poor, and public safety measures such as patrolling the streets at night. At the same time, it attacks secularists and moderates. It now attacks sites that are venerated by Sufi Muslims such as tombs of figures considered saints. Islamic groups in Libya appear to have come full circle.[25]

PART III: WEST AFRICA

Geographically, West Africa is composed of two ecological reasons. The northern zone is approximately the region between the Sahara Desert and the rainforest zone which extends from the Atlantic Ocean to this northern grassland zone. In turn, the upper section of this northern more arid part of what is often called the Sudanic or northern savanna belt is called the Sahel. In general, this grassland belt which has been a historically cultural transmission route extends from the Atlantic Ocean on the west to the Red Sea on the east. It is 300 to 500 miles in width and encompasses the countries of Mauritania, Senegal, Gambia, Niger, Burkina Faso, Chad, and Sudan. The Ethiopian highlands are an extension of this ecological region. The northern sections of Nigeria and Cameroon and the western part of Guinea are also included in this zone. Small sections of the rainforest West African states of Liberia, Sierra Leone, Togo, the Ivory Coast, Ghana, and Benin have similar topographical features. The West African rainforest belt includes the above mentioned countries as well as Equatorial Guinea and the northern sectors of Cameroon and Nigeria.

The Sudanic zone is predominantly Muslim. It has undergone several stages of Islamization. It also has come to his region in several ways. Military conquest, trade and economic links, missionary work, and expansion through family and lineage connections have all played a role.

Muslim expansion arrived with trading links initially after 700. Between 800 and 1550, West Africa was a source of much of the gold specie used in currency in the Middle East and Europe. The various states and empires which arose in the Sudanic belt gained their economic rationale and much of their wealth as middlemen between traders from North Africa who passed through these transit areas so as to obtain gold from sources in what is now Burkina

Faso, Ivory Coast, and Ghana. These traders would bring finished goods as well as salt mined in the Sahara to trade for the gold. Ivory was also collected from the south as well as blue dye, rhinoceros horn, and slaves. The middlemen states would collect transit tolls on items going both north and south. The trade occurred in various ways including the "silent trade" previously described. When gold and silver specie began to arrive in large amounts after 1550 from the western hemisphere, the economic rationale declined. After 1000, military conquest through puritanical Berber orders such as the Almoravids and Almohads played a role. Military action by Morocco at the western end and the Ottoman Empire at the eastern end also led to the spread of Islam. Reform jihads (known as the Fulani Jihads due to the prominence of one group) also led to expansion in the eighteenth and nineteenth centuries. Traders from the area who utilized economic and lineage kinship links primarily from Mali also spread Islam to the southern sections of this region after 1500. (see the following chapters and the introduction).

Chapter 4

MALI

Of all the Sudanic states, Mali has had the most prominent connections to Islam over the centuries. It is the repository of Islamic learning on such fabled cities as Timbuktu and Jenne. Various dialects of its language, Mande, were used by the dyula traders who spread Islam throughout the region over the centuries. It was the center of a legendary empire in the Middle Ages in which Islam played a significant role.[1] Islamic brotherhoods — Sufi and otherwise — have long been active in the country. In 2012 and 2013, it was the site of radical Islamic groups who seized control of much of the country and would have taken control of all of Mali if not for French intervention. Islam reached the country from the north and east. During the first millennium, the introduction of the camel reduced the barrier which the Sahara had posed between North Africa and West Africa. As a consequence, the Sahara was similar to an ocean with river sites and oases being the equivalent of ports and entreports in this ocean.[2]

The second enabling factor was the partial Arabization of North Africa. The arrival of the Banu Hilal and the Banu Sulaym had the effect after 1000 of pushing the newly-converted Berbers south. In reaction the Berbers and Tuaregs (the central and southern Berbers) consolidated their political status and formed confederations. The most prominent was the the Sanhaja group.[3] The brotherhood of this group — the Almoravids — helped to put an end to Mali's predecessor, the semi-pagan empire of Ghana. Various groups of nomadic pastoralists (the Berber/Tuareg groups and later the Fulani of mixed Berber/Black African descent) would trade with and raid their Black African neighbors. These activities would be often commingled with messianic Islam. In the early centuries (before 1500), the starting points for peaceful and warlike expeditions alike were Andoghast and Sillijamasa now in Southern Morocco and Mauritania respectively.[4] In later centuries, the starting points were Ghadames, Ghat, and Agades in the central Maghrib and Tripoli in the eastern Maghrib –all of which were accessible to the Sudanic belt including Mali.[5]

The "ports" in this "ocean" such as Timbuktu, Jenne, and Gao, the original capital of Mali, were centers not only for commerce but for Islamic learning. Timbuktu, in particular, was famous for both its mosque as well as its university of Sankore. To a lesser extent, most cities had Muslim centers. Even the non-Muslim empire of Ghana had a twin capital (Kumbi-Saleh); Kumbi was the administrative center while Saleh was the residence for Muslim merchants. The Sufi orientation of some Muslim buildings including the tombs of saints (anathema to orthodox fundamentalist Muslims) became objects of destruction to radicals during the recent Muslim takeover.[6]

Another significant factor is the centrality of Mali in this area and in Islam is demographics. The largest ethnic/linguistic group (along with Hausa) in the grassland area is the Mande/Mende/Mandingo/Malinka group which extends from the Atlantic Ocean to Lake Chad. It is devoutly Muslim as is the Berber/Tuareg group. Mali has the largest group of Berbers/Tuaregs in the west Sudanic area. It was this group which founded Timbuktu.[7]

By 1100, Mande-speakers called Dyula or Jyula had become the dominant group of traders in the southern zone of the region. They were not only traders but also craftsmen. By 1200, they had entered the rainforest and were trading in Kola nuts in that region with people who controlled the gold fields in Upper Volta (now Burkina Faso) as well as the Akan peoples in what is now the northern part of Ghana. Over the centuries, they were conduits of Islam to Senegal, Guinea, and the Ivory Coast as well as northern Nigeria and Cameroon.[8]

The ancient empire of Mali whose summit was between 1235 and 1468 was key to this dissemination. Its most famous ruler was Mansa Musa who reigned in the early 14th century and was famous for his wealth. A devout Muslim, his pilgrimage to Mecca which passed through Cairo witnessed such a huge expenditure of gold that the market was depressed for years. This reign and succeeding reigns witnessed a mass construction of mosques and attendance at these Mosques became mandatory.[9]

Despite these developments, Islam in 1800 was still primarily observed by upper classes and in urban areas. The mass of people who lived in the countryside often practiced traditional beliefs and practices. In addition, many nominal Muslims commingled Islam with traditional beliefs in a syncretistic manner.[10]

Nonetheless, Islam continued to spread as Islamic teachers often accompanied traders followed by jurists. These Islamic jurists and teachers continued to travel south even after the empires declined. They established schools and mosques from their home bases from Mali and other Sudanic states especially in what are now Burkina Faso, Ivory Coast, and Togo.[11] Sometimes, these Dyula traders from Mali and related areas were also jurists trained in Timbuktu. By 1700, there were hundreds of settlements of traders, teachers in Guinea, the general term for rainforest West Africa.[12]

Nevertheless, in some ways this was a period of stagnation in Mali as elsewhere as the gradual conversion of peasants often meant an accommodation with pre-existing beliefs. Perhaps inevitably, a reaction set in and the period after 1700 witnessed two developments which were to have long-lasting effects. First, was the revival of ancient religious brotherhoods such as the Quadiriyya and the arrival of new indigenous brotherhoods such as the Murridiyya and the Tijaniyya. Their aim was to purify Islam. Some were a-political which is the usual approach of Sufism; others were militant.[13]

The other reaction came on the reform in a series of reform movements which became Islamic revolutions in the 18th and especially the 19th century. These movements were aimed at what was considered individuals who were backsliders to the point of apostasy so that these movements were in fact jihads that aimed at restoring Islam to its original pristine state. They were identified with the Fulani people of West Africa so that they are also called the Fulani Revolutions. After relatively minor revolutions in Futa Toro in 1725 in what is now Senegal and Futa Jalon in 1776 is what is now present-day Guinea, the major revolutions took place in what is now Hausaland in northern Nigeria and in adjacent areas and in what now Mali. The first, led by Uthman dan Fodio, affected millions of people as Hausa is the major trading language today in West Africa in 1804 and 1810-12. (It will be discussed more fully in the following section on Nigeria).[14]

The first iihad that occurred in what is now Mali had profound impact as it helped to spread Islam from the towns to the countryside and from the upper classes to the common people. In so doing, Islam was transformed from an elite faith to a religion of the masses. Inspired by the Sokoto Jihad, Seku Ahmadu (also known as Ahmadu Lobbo) spent the years 1811-1818 leading his followers against the corrupt practices that had crept into cities in the middle Niger region (now southwest Mali near the present capital of Bamako) as well as neighboring states under pagan rule. The state which utilized the assistance of other Fulani ultimately extended up to Timbuktu so that by the time of his death, much of Mali and areas were under his control in state was called Masina after the initial capital which was later replaced by Hamdullah (Praise be to the Lord). Advised by a clerical Fulani council, he attempted to govern all of his subjects according to the Qur'an). He banned the sale and consumption of tobacco. He went further and restricted alcohol and chocolate. The law dictated by the Sunna precepts was to be based on strict observance of the Maliki law code. Women were segregated; religious judges (quadi) administered the law; and music and dancing was forbidden. He constructed six hundred new madrassas or religious schools. He set up a pattern for theocratic control of a state that was to endure for half a century. He even declared himself the 12th Caliph of Islam.[15]

He and his successors were opposed by the Kinta, the priestly caste that was allied with the dyula traders who had made accommodation with pagan non-Muslim regimes a part of their approach for half a millennium. Lobbo's successors gradually moved away from the tradition of Islamic control and education and became more accommodating. It was this tendency that caused it to become the object of the new jihad. It was led by a man called Al-Hajj Umar, a Fulani from Futa Toro who joined the more militant order of the Tijaniyya — the order originally from North Africa that had its most prominent success in West Africa. After some years in Sokoto as well as Futa Toro and Futa Jalon, he launched his jihad as a representative of the Tijaniyya. His opponents were not only the remaining pagan states but backsliders in which he grouped Masina along with Kunta clerics and the Quadiriyya order all of which he termed as accomodationists. Securing arms from British and French sources, he had become the dominant military power in the western Sudan –ranging from the Senegal to Niger regions including Mali. Eventually, he overreached himself and was defeated and killed while besieging Masina in 1864.[16]

His successor was Samori who was Mande-speaking not Fulani but was influenced by clerics from Futa Toro and Futa Jallon He established headquarters on the Volta River but ultimately his vast empire included much of the territory from Senegal to Guinea He soon extended his empire to include much of the Niger River including parts of Mali. He developed an efficient military machine including arms factories as well an effective information and communications service. He incorporated the lands of other Islamic leaders who in Mali and elsewhere had declared jihads. During his 16 year rule and opposition to the onset of French colonialism, he engaged in widespread conversion efforts to Islam and opened mosques and schools even in the smallest villages. Islamic law was introduced throughout the state.[17]

Ultimately, he was opposed by the dyula-linked ulama class who had shown greater tolerance for non-believers — a policy that he opposed. Many of them now allied themselves with the French, and Samori was ultimately defeated.[18] Samori and his predecessors have left a mixed legacy in Mali. Although respected for their piety and bravery, it is believed that attacks on other Muslims and native Malian rulers led to widespread damage and loss of life, and eventually weakened Muslim and indigenous resistance to colonial rule.[19]

The subsequent advantage in Islam in Mali went back to the Islamic establishment which traditionally had more tolerant, more syncretic, and less fundamentalist. Consequently, it worked with and was supported by colonial authorities during French rule when it was known as French Soudan. Initially suspicious especially of the brotherhoods as secret conspirators, the French attitude underwent a transformation. WWI indicated that the West African Muslims had remained loyal and had been courageous soldiers (the exception had been Sanusiyya rebellions in Chad). The services of the dyula were utilized as intermediaries and Muslim institutions and functionaries were supported — it as a marriage of convenience which lasted until the 1950's when young Muslims educated abroad began to challenge the establishment as too inclined to support the status quo including the colonial system.[20]

Even earlier, the French had developed the concept of "Black Islam" which might be used to reconcile Muslims to "civilization" which was defined as French values as a form of assimilation. The Sahel countries considered Islamic such as Mauritania, Senegal, Mali, and Niger were benefitted from the discouragement of Christian missionaries. The dyula and members of the brotherhoods were assisted by a Service of Service Affairs which supported Islamic activities. These activities included missionary activity in the south of Mali which converted remaining animists to Islam. In this way, the Islamic presence was strengthened during the colonial period. Establishment Islam supported collaboration in the name of self-interest. The members of the establishment even invoked the model of dissimulation based on the example of secret Muslims in Spain in Granada after its fall. This is the doctrine associated with Iranian Shia and rarely by Sunna.[21]

Independence in 1960 brought at first, a hostile environment. The newly-installed president, Modibo Keita, attacked all associations including Muslim ones deemed "dangerous." After 1968, when Keita was overthrown, the situation changed. It became socially acceptable in Mali to identify oneself as Muslim without being considered anti-national or "dangerous." For a while, radical Wahhabis supported by Saudi Arabians and Sufis appeared to be united in the desire for salvation in the hereafter that could be related to the desire for a better life here on earth. It should be emphasized that these developments were in the Mande-speakers residents in Mali in the south and central sections of Mali. As will be seen, the feelings of the Tuareg Berbers in the northern part of the country differed.[22]

During the period of 1968-2008, there appeared a consensus among different schools of Islam. The government sponsored umbrella organization the Malian Association for Islam's Unity and Progress. In contrast to the riots which occurred in Bamako at various mosques, Muslims were now encouraged to attend the nearest mosque with regard to the imam's denomination. The closing of some Islamic schools was replaced by the encouragement of schools both operated by native reformers called "Azharists" who cooperated with the Sufi influenced zawiya schools. The Wahhabi and Sufi teachers saw themselves in spite of differences as members of the same team. Intramural violence among Muslims was discouraged. Television, radio video cassettes, even the internet was used to broadcast some Friday prayers and the program the "Muslim Hours" broadcast in Mande. These programs also broadcast in non-Mande languages were explained in modern terms by often telegenic spokesmen dressed in modern garb. Both literate and non-literate societies were thereby reached. As a result, Islamization has increased. At the same time, Islam was incorporated into the national mainstream. Secular subjects, in this manner, were introduced into the curriculum such as geography and science so that Qur'anic schools were competitive with French-run schools.[23]

This unity emerged in spite of doctrinal differences, Younger craftsmen and traders unlike the majority of collaborationist Wahhabis, have opposed Western education, practice gender separation to the point of not even shaking hands, and encouraged the wearing of veils for women and beards for men as quranic necessities. At the other end of the spectrum, more moderate Muslims maintain that they are part of a "new age" which recognizes gender equality and the participation of women in society. The Malian state did encourage modernization, but, at the same time, maintained Islamic ties, which included the joining of the first international Islamic Conference held in Rabat. This conference led to the founding of the OIC or Organization of Islamic Conference in which Mali remains a member.[24]

The years since 2011 have seen a breakdown in the previous balance. The consensus that Islam can be a national tool by welcoming all shades of opinion has collapsed. The attitude of collaboration was more typical of southern and central Mali than the Tuareg North, In Mali as in the other Sahel countries (Mauritania, Niger, Chad) there is cleavage between the Black African south and the Berber/Tuareg north. In recent years, the Tuareg/Berber has adopted a radical Islam view along with secessionist aspirations along with age-old antipathy between nomadic pastoralist and settled farmers and urban dwellers.[24]

In consequence, Mali has become the epicenter for Islamic radicals who have spread south from North Africa. Already facing insurrection from in the north, Mali was thrown into chaos after a military coup in March 2012. The rebellion then became a threat to the whole country as government troops were defeated. Originally it involved a somewhat more moderate group of Tauregs who felt marginalized in a rather alien polity beset in recent by accusations of corruption and the drug trade (anathema to many Muslims). They sought autonomy or outside independence as an independent state or part of larger political entity which would encompass the Berber sections of several states. Gradually, the political arm of this group, Ansar Dine, [25] was pushed aside as the rebellion metastasized. Al Qaeda in the Islamic Maghrib, active in North Africa (AQIM) which had grown exponentially since its founding in 2005 was joined by The Salafist Group for Preaching and Combat. AQIM has become the leading Islamist militant group in both West and North Africa. It has made millions through kidnapping and extortion.[26]

Offshoots of AQIM abound. Maktar Belnakti, a local leader, left AQIM to form his own organizations now active in Mali, Masked Men and Signed in Blood. Another radical group (also active in North Africa and Niger), The Movement for Monotheism and Jihad (MUJAO) is also active in Mali. By April 2012, it had joined two Tuareg groups, the National Movement for the Liberation of Azawad (MNLA — Azawad is the name for the proposed Taureg state in northern Mali) as well as the aforementioned Ansar Dine. By the summer, these groups had been joined by Sons of the Islamic Sahara Movement for Justice which operates in next-door Niger, western Libya, and southern Algeria. It should be noted that the fall of Kaddafi in Libya in 2011 left a number of groups with a great many arms. It was even reported that the Nigerian terrorist group, Boko Haram, had sent in armed battalions. As these groups often regroup (in August 2013, for example, the Masked Men and MUJAO had partially assumed new identities), they are difficult to track.[27]

By fall 2012, the Berber groups were dominated by the radical Islamists. This development was perhaps inevitable as porous borders combined with Mali"s central location made it easy for other radical groups to send in supplies and reinforcements from Mauritania, Niger, Algeria, Libya, and Nigeria. In the spring of 2013, French troops reoccupied northern Mali. More precisely, they liberated the towns and cities. However, some of these extremists still exist in the countryside and can be reinforced at any time from their sanctuaries in neighboring countries.[28]

They left behind much damage especially in such historic cities as Gao, Jenne, and Timbuktu. Although Timbuktu was initially protected by the Tuareg Berbers with whom it had a long connection, the immunity did not lost long once they were pushed aside, and much destruction of holy sites took place. The reason was that these holy sites were connected in general to Sufism and to the moderate Quadariyya brotherhood. In Timbuktu, this was illustrated by the destruction of the sacred Sidya Yahya mosque. There was also damage to the ancient Islamic university of Sankore.[29] Gao, the largest city in the region and the proposed capital of this new state of Azawad, also suffered damage in part because it had gained the reputation of being a somewhat secular city. Tombs of Sufi saints were damaged and tomb of Askia Muhammad, the devout emperor of Songhay, the successor state of Mali, and the surrounding ancient mosque was destroyed.[30] When the French withdrew, they were replaced in 2013 by an international peacekeeping force of 12,000 troops sent by the African Union.[31]

Today, Mali faces a fractured future. It includes in its northern half a discontent group whose unhappiness is exaggerated by extremist internal and external forces. Without assistance from abroad, it faces the possibility of dismemberment for religious as well as ethnic reasons. This is unfortunate as Mali and its people played a key role in the Islamization of the region.

Chapter 5

NIGERIA

Islam has been a dominant force in Nigeria since the 12th century. Composed of Bornu in the Northeast and Hausaland in the North central and Northwest of the country, the Muslims constitute about half of the population of Nigeria. (The Hausa are the largest ethnic group in the continent's most populous country, and Hausa is the "lingua franca" in West Africa because of the trading tradition of the group). Bornu located currently on the southwest shore was originally centered in the in the northeast of Lake Chad. Its main ethnic group, the Kanuri, had converted by the mid-12th century. Its conversion came from the eastern trading route from Tripoli to Lake Chad as well as from Cyrenaica and Fezzan. It also received Islamic influences via the state of Wadai in what is now the border of Sudan and Chad,[1]

The state of Kanem-Bornu lasted in one form or another for about a millennium. It had become so devout that by the mid-13th century, a ruler was making the pilgrimage to Mecca and the rulers tried to convert their neighbors. Due to attacks from a rival group, the Kanuri relocated their state to its present location during the 14th century. During the fifteenth century, the ruler assumed the title of caliph ("successor to the prophet"). At its height, around 1600, Bornu was the southern terminus of the eastern route of the Trans-Saharan trade. At this time, this was the dominant route as the western and central routes had been disrupted by the Moroccan defeat of the last great Sudanic Empire, Songhay, and the territory had become fragmented. Due to its wealth, Bornu exerted influence including the spread of Islam on its neighbors.[2] The ruler or mai supported religious scholars and sent students to study at Al-Azhar where a separate section was established for Bornu. By 1600, Sharia was considered the law of the land. The Quadiriyya brotherhood, imams, and religious teachers were exempted from taxation. By 1800, Islam had penetrated so deeply into society that unlike its neighbor states which had become nominally Muslim, it had affected daily life of most people of all classes from birth to death.[3]

Bornu was a target of the 19th century Fulani jihads as its ruler was accused of unlawful Islamic taxation as well as bribery and corruption. Although there was a degree of syncretism which occasionally involved human sacrifice, Bornu, due to its long history of affiliation with Islam, withstood the Fulani jihad. Annexation by the British did not greatly affect the status of Islam as the British practiced indirect rule in Northern Nigeria. Accordingly, the mai of Bornu retained his traditional role. The latter included the right of appointment of Islamic judges or quadi who could administer sharia-based law. Since independence, the Islamic status of Bornu has reflected the position of other Muslim states in Nigeria.[4]

The Hausa community of Nigeria is the most numerous group in West Africa. There are 40 million speakers in Nigeria and 12 million speak it in neighboring countries particularly Niger and Cameroon. Several million other West Africans speak it as a second language.[5] In addition, the Fulani who are now intermingled with the Hausa have over 15 million in numbers in Nigeria alone (they are also spread throughout West Africa, in part because they are or were pastoralists and partly because they led the Islamic Jihads in the 18th and 19th centuries.[6] When one adds the Kanuri of Bornu (now called Borno) plus other Muslims in Nigeria, it is easy to see why the Muslim population is close to if not the majority in Nigeria.[7] Since Independence, the majority of the presidents (with a few exceptions such as the present incumbent) have been either Fulani or Hausa.[8]

The Hausa lived in city-states as early as the 11th century. By the end of 14th century, Islam had become prominent in the two largest cities, Kano and Katsina. By the 15th century, it had penetrated most of Hausaland via dyula traders. In addition, Hausaland had been tributary to Muslim empires such as Mali and Songhay and some of the Hausa states were tributary to Bornu. By the end of the 16th century, a pattern had been established. Even though Islam had become integrated into the social, cultural, and religious life of the Hausa, it assumed a hybrid character. The rulers of these city-states had Islamic practices for their judicial systems. However, the kings/sultans of these city-states often oscillated between Islam and traditional belief and sometimes even pre-Islamic paganism. As a result, orthodox Muslim beliefs were practiced along with the veneration of saints and the belief in jinns.[9]

This custom was prevalent even in the most Islamic of Hausa cities, Katsina. The rival of Kano in terms of wealth and commerce as a southern terminus for the route from Tripoli, this city was so pious that it had elected as the king a Muslim cleric at the end of the 15th century.[10] Nevertheless, even in Katsina the traditional beliefs or bori were incorporated into Islam and some obeisance was made to priest-chiefs who practiced the bori system. The accommodation existed not only in Katsina, but in the other traditional Hausa cities of Kano, Gobir, Rano, Daura, Zaria, and Bauchi which were part of the original Hausa city-states or Habe.[11] Another 7 city states where Hausa had replaced the original language were Kebbi, Nupe, Gwari or Borgu, Yauri, Yoruba (the place not the southwestern group), and Kwararafa. Although not considered part of the original core, some of these states such as Kebbi and Nupe were of considerable size and importance. They also practiced religious syncretism in which Islam comingled with bori and other traditional beliefs.[12]

By 1800, a number of more orthodox Muslims especially the Fulani who had settled in rural areas of Hausaland were dissatisfied with this situation. Under the leadership of a scholar-cleric, Uthman dan Fodio, they launched a jihad against these "impure" regimes. Beginning in 1804, against Gobir, these regimes including the ruling emirs or sultans and their clerical advisors were accused of corruption, practicing pagan beliefs including Bori, and imposing un-Islamic taxes. By 1812, Hausaland had been overrun and a new state had been established, the sultanate of Sokoto, with the former cities as tributaries often under Fulani rule. The old Hausa bureaucracy was retained, and the new rulers gradually came to speak Hausa through intermarriage. It expanded beyond the traditional borders of Hausaland with the state of Bornu being the only state which resisted successfully.[13] The son and successor of Uthman dan Fodio assumed the title of Caliph. During the following decades a deeper belief and practice in Islam spread. Mosques and schools opened in both rural and urban areas. In spite of their own past militancy, the Quadiriyya order was supported as a tool by the Sokoto authorities.[14] Agriculture and the crafts increased in part due to a supply of slaves obtained from raiding the non-Muslim south, Increased production plus greater security led to greater commerce with both the trans-Sahara and forest routes.[15] At that time, the sphere of influence of the Caliphate included parts of Niger, Burkina Faso, and Benin as well as part of Cameroon. When Britain, France, and Germany divided up the Caliphate in 1903, Britain took Hausaland proper while France took the first three and Germany the latter.[16]

During the colonial period, Northern Nigeria (mostly Hausaland and Bornu) became a showcase for indirect rule. With exception of the abolition of slavery and introducing British legal precepts for homicide, the traditional rulers retained their judicial roles.[17] This system involved the continuance of Sharia for private and domestic law while the British system was used for criminal law. The rulers maintained the right to appoint traditional judges or "alkalis." The emirs who ruled under the Sultan of Sokoto and their subordinate emirs, for example, were considered both spiritual and administrative officials. Christian educations were acceptable but Christian missionaries were often not encouraged. Secular subjects were added to the school curriculum but the Qur'an was not abolished.[18]

The colonial period actually strengthened Islam as British officers kept the peace so that Muslim preachers could spread the word in previous remote and lawless places. Improvements in telecommunications and transportation allowed Islamic preachers to reach people by radio and motor vehicle. In some cases, the British assisted the spread of Islam under the indigenous emirs by introducing Sharia into non-Muslim areas.[19]

The close relationship between religion and civil society was evident at Independence in 1960. The Nigerian Peoples Party which represented the north was headed by Ahmadu Bello, the Sarduna or Sultan of Sokoto, and the epitome of Muslim establishment, while Sir Abubakar Balewa, the first Prime Minister of the Federation of Nigeria, was a Muslim from the north. The country was divided into three parts with the Sultan of Sokoto as the nominal head of the northern Muslim region.[20]

Since Independence there have been both intramural conflicts among Muslims and conflicts between Muslims and Christians, There have feuds between the conservative ulama and those directly subservient to the federal government and the ruler of Sokoto. There were also clashes between the Quadiriyya and the Tijaniyya orders. The first was the more conservative establishment order supported by the Sultan of Sokoto while the latter was supported by the emir of Kano, the largest city.[21] Another intramural dispute was between Sunni orthodox and Sufis. The Gran Kadi of the north, the chief religious official, Abubakar Gummi, was on the first side. Gummi and his followers allied with the fundamentalist organization, The Yan Uzala, and the Muslim university group, the Muslim Students Society attacked the brotherhoods as out of touch. They all wanted a greater role for Islam within the state. Others claim to be the spiritual and intellectual descendants of Uthman dan Fodio which sought to preserve his puritanical legacy such as the Society for the Victory of Islam. So diverse is Nigerian Islam that there are factions within factions. Both the Quadiriyya and the Tijaniyya brotherhoods have reformist and traditional factions.[22]

The relationship between Muslims and Christians and Islam and society as a whole has been an ongoing issue in Nigeria since Independence. The decision to join Islamic organizations has been very controversial. Nigeria's decision to join the Organization of the Islamic Conference provoked riots in 1986 as it was taken as a sign of creeping Islamization. Nigeria officially withdrew in 1991, although the OIC still considers Nigeria a member if unofficial. In the meantime, Nigeria belongs to a number of Islamic organizations such as the International Islamic Organization and the International Islamic Federation of Student Organizations. The other ongoing issue is the role of Islamic law in a multi-confessional country which has no official religion. At independence, the various emirs could appoint judges. In addition, there was a Northern Region Sharia Court of Appeal. The chaos during the early days led to the abolition of the court and the emir's power of appointment.[23]

Finally, there has been a source of strife in millennial and messianic movements which have arisen from time to time. In the 1970's, for example, Alhaji Mujammadu Marwa known as Maitatsine campaigned against the corruption of Nigerian Islam as well Nigerian society as a whole. He proclaimed himself greater than the Prophet and amassed a huge following. They engaged in riots throughout the 1980's with the largest being in Kano which took the life of the founder. In the nineties, his place was taken by Sheik Ibrahim al-Zakzady (a Shiite) who challenged "secular" government and encouraged his followers to forcibly take over the mosques, Ensuing clashed with the authorities by his followers led to his arrest and imprisonment.[24] The greatest source of conflict since Independence in 1960 has been Christian-Muslim sectarian strife. Only three presidents in the past 54 years have been Christian including the current occupant, Goodluck Jonathan.[25] Even before the rise of Boko Haram, the current Islamic terrorist group,[26] there has been a tragic history of violence over questionable census statistics —always a potentially controversial issue in a closely divided country. The reaction to a coup led by an Igbo non-Muslim general in January 1966 led to widespread violence in the north against Christians and Igbo that was estimated to be 10,000 to 30,000 and the departure of perhaps one million from the north. A countercoup in July, 1966 by Northerners led to the Biafran secession (1967-70) and a tragic loss of life which may have totaled over 1,000,000.[27]

Continued violence in the north did not abate after the end of the Biafran war. After 1980, Muslims were especially incensed by the arrival of Christian evangelicals and missionaries. Rampages occurred in both urban and rural areas. In 1982, there were a series of attacks against churches in Kano. This action was followed by attacks in Kaduna state against the YMCA and the burning down by 150 students of the chapel at Ahmadu Bello University in Zaria as well as five mosques on the other end.[28] In 1988, disagreement over state elections led to pitched battles between Christian and Muslim students. Further, a proposed visit from a Christian fundamentalist preacher caused riots in Kano in 1990. Communal violence throughout the nineteen nineties annually took scores or hundreds of lives.[29]

The conflict has continued to the present. In 2000, the adoption of Sharia for use in certain domestic cases in northern Nigeria over Christian objections resulted in the deaths of hundreds in subsequent violence.[30]

Violence has spread beyond the northern region in recent years. In February 2002 more than 100 people were killed in ethnic violence with sectarian overtones in Lagos between Hausa and ethnic Yoruba.[31] In that same month, Muslims rioted over a Miss World content which offended Muslim sensibilities over modesty.[32]

During this past decade, there has been a cycle of attack followed by retaliation between Christians and Muslims. In May 2004, attacks on Christians in Kano led to Christian reprisal in central Nigeria and the loss of over 200 Muslim lives. This attack was followed by yet another Christian reprisal which also took over 200 lives in the southern port of Onitsha.[33]

For a period of time, rising oil prices and the resultant relative prosperity for Nigeria tamped down violence. Since 2009, however, communal violence has risen. This is partly due to the efforts of Boko Haram (discussed later) but also due to migration of Muslims to other parts of the country. The violence has not always been caused by Muslims as Christian extremism has also increased. Jos, in particular, in central Nigeria has become a flashpoint. Christian gangs in that city have often rioted so that in 2010 alone hundreds if people died in Christian-Muslim clashes.[34]

There are other causes for conflict. The militant organization, the Movement for the Emancipation of the Niger Delta (MEND) has been active on land and off the coast in Nigeria where piracy has dramatically increased. The drilling companies have been accused of corruption and are also charged with the complicity of officials not returning a fair share of royalties. However, the greatest loss of life has come through communal violence which continues to this day. The most recent election between Muhammadu Buhari, a Muslim from the north, and the ultimate winner, Goodwill Jonathan, a Christian from the south, caused violent protest from Buhari's supporters. Ultimately these protests took over 800 lives.[35]

In the last few years, however, it is in the activities of the Boko Haram (literally the Congregation of Tradition for the Proselytization and Jihad) that have caused widespread destruction and loss of life. Although based in Nigeria, its activities have spilled over into neighboring Cameroon and Niger both of whom have large Hausa Muslim populations. This organization has been responsible for over 10,000 deaths between 2001 and 2014 (it continues to this day) particularly after it ratcheted up its attacks after 2010 when it declared it was on a jihad. It attributes its inspiration to seventies messianic Maitatsine and has exploited rampant corruption, poverty, and unemployment. It operates throughout the country but especially in the north Muslim provinces of Borno(Bornu), Adamawa, and Yobe. It has attacked both Christian and Muslim targets deemed to be "corrupt." These targets include schools, churches, police stations, and military quarters. States of emergency have been declared in Borno, Adamawa, Kaduna, Bauchi, Yobe, and Kano.[36]

The violent attacks have not been limited to the north. The federal capital, Abuja, in central Nigeria, has been attacked several times since 2010 with a stress on military and police targets. Attacks have also occurred in the south. Repeatedly, it has organized prison breaks as a recruiting tool. It has reportedly split into three factions with the most aggressive, Ansaru, being linked to AQIM (Al-Qaeda in the Islamic Maghrib), and, as was indicated earlier, is believed to have sent battalians to support the Islamic uprising in Mali.[37]

Currently, Nigeria has many problems. The outbreaks in the Oil Rivers region in the southeast over fair division of oil profits by MENG and the related issue of piracy which is now worse than in Somalia and a threat to international shipping has already been recounted.[38] Certainly corruption and poverty is an ongoing issue.

Overall, however, it is the sectarian divide which remains the biggest obstacle. Although Nigeria has dozens of ethnic groups and over a hundred separate languages and dialects, it is its major three fold division which bedevils unity. The British cobbled together an artificial entity with three divisions (although officially there are now three dozen states) which have different traditions, cultures, and languages. The south and the Yoruba, the Igbo and the southeast, and the Hausa/Fulani/Kanuri and the north have separate histories and sometimes different points of view (even with the new division of three dozen states designed to reduce regional consciousness). Over this divide, there is now a Muslim/Christian divide between the Islamic north and the Christian south/southeast. The question now is: will Nigeria break up due to sectarian differences as was the case of Sudan or will it forge a new identity which supersedes communal differences?

PART IV: EAST AFRICA

Chapter 6

SOMALIA

Islam came to East Africa in two stages. It arrived via trade between 750 and 1500. Then Muslims gradually penetrated inland. The bulk of Islamic conversion (at least south of present-day Somalia)) came after 1800; in Somalia the conversion rate began around 1000. The coast from what is Mogadishu in central Somalia to central Mozambique saw the arrival of Islam with trade. The city-states along the coast were the middlemen between the interior of Africa and the outside world. During their heyday, the northern coast states traded primarily with the Lake States for ivory in return for goods from the Middle East and the Indian Ocean littoral, the central states traded for iron and copper from the Congo basin to the Middle east and countries from Middle East to Southeast Asia, and the southern cities traded for gold with the Empire centered in Zimbabwe as intermediaries with the outside world.[1]

The section of the East African Coast from the Red Sea to the Horn of Africa down the Indian Ocean Coast to what is now the approximate southern coast of Somalia is historically important as a trading site that dates back at least 2000 B. C. It was known as the land of Punt in ancient times and its inhabitants traded will various areas of the ancient world including the Mediterranean area as well as the Middle East and were identified with the bringers of spices such as frankincense and myrrh. The present day-inhabitants are a branch of the Afro-Asiatic group identified with North Africa and the present-day Sudan and Ethiopia. The ancestors of what became the Somali arrived in the first millennium B.C.E.[2]

Islam came to what is now Somalia as early as the 7th century when Muslim refugees found sanctuary across the Red Sea in the port of Adulis than under the control of Axum. There were a series of coastal states from the 8th century which embraced Islam such as Ifat, Adat, Ajurran, Mujaeerteen, and Olbia sultanates. They did advance inland for trade, but much of the period between 1000 and 1500 saw a struggle between these Islamic states and Christian Ethiopia.[3]

After 1500, a larger Muslim group, the Galla, now called the Oromo, came to occupy much of what today is Ethiopia (at least its southern and southeastern sections). Most of what was to become the Somali nation was in the hinterland subdivided unto pastoral clans –the chief being the Darood, the Isaak, the Hawayie, and the Dir and still is. It is not entirely a coincidence that the clan identities correspond to the secessionist states (the Isaak in Somaliland and part of the Darood in Puntland, and the Dir in Somaliland and Djibouti; the Hawayie and part of the Darood along with two smaller clans are based in Somalia proper). At the same time, the port cities of Merca, Barawa, and Mogadishu emerged as Islamic port cities and gradually became predominately Somali in nature. The medieval Ajurran confederacy was the first that was both Islamic and Somali. Its proximity to these cities (the hinterland of what sailors and navigators called the Benadir Coast) reinforced both the ethnicity and Islamic identity of the Somali. Nevertheless, the majority of the emerging Somali idenily were pastoralists who wandered among what is today Somalia (including its two secessionist states of Somaliland and Puntland), the present state of Djibouti, the Ogaden region of Ethiopia, and Northeastern Kenya. The degree of Islamization of these nomadic and semi-nomadic groups varied and was often intermingled with traditional beliefs. As in other parts of Africa, Islam at this time was often concentrated among the ruling elite and in the cities.[4]

Mogadishu which typified this situation, before it declined somewhat during Portuguese and later Omani rule, still experienced a golden age. It was called the city of Islam because of its many mosques with its famous minarets. Its wealth supported this display. Its merchants traded gold, ivory, and wax to India and the Far East for which they received cloth and spices. The huge internal markets sold milk, wheat, barley, meat, and fruit among other items. It had a very prosperous textile industry which sold its product throughout the Middle East.[5]

The spread of Islam in the interior of Somalia was due in part to the religious orders of the Quadiriyya and the Salihiyya. Both founded tarika settlements throughout Somalia. The first was perhaps more typically Sufi. The leaders or Shaykhs promoted a humble pure lifestyle and emphasized the teacher of Islam and Arabic — the latter as a means of teaching the former. The Quadariyya supported an identity based on Islam rather than kinship. It encouraged Somalis of various clans to live together as brothers and engage in agricultural pursuits and communal study and worship. The brotherhood accepted (as elsewhere) traditional folk beliefs such as spiritual intercession of holy men and emphasized personal devotion on the part of the devotee. By such measures it gained widespread acceptance for itself and for Islam. More militant was the Salihiyya. It supported holy war or jihad against both the Christian invaders as it viewed western imperialist as well as the historical enemy of Ethiopia as well as Muslims who aided them. It adamantly opposed the inclusion of anything such as traditional beliefs that would "corrupt" Islam.

This attitude of resistance to anything that was not pure Islam was to show itself in the career of Sayyid Muhammad called by his western opponents, "the Mad Mullah of Somaliland." In the last two decades of the nineteenth century, the Somali nation was under siege. The British occupied Kenya including its Somali areas. Ethiopia under Menelik was expansionist and occupied parts of western parts of Somalia including the city of Harar and the Ogaden desert.[6] Finally, between 1885 and 1900, the rest of Somalia was divided among Great Britain, France, and Italy. Italy took the largest portion in what is today Somalia (she was not actively opposed by the other two countries as she had just been defeated by the Emperor of Ethiopia — the first defeat of a European power by an African state during the Partition of Africa and had lost Eritrea, and the bulk of Somalia was her consolation). Great Britain took the section which today corresponds to "Puntland" and "Somaliland" while France took what is today Djibouti.[7] It was this background which led to the jihad of Sayyid Muhammad which combined religion with cultural nationalism. In so doing, he defined Somali identity as being in part derived from religion (and language and culture) as opposed to clan or sub-clan identity. In a sense, he was the first pan-Somali nationalist. Not too surprisingly, therefore, he was a leader or shaykh of the militant Salihiyya brotherhood. His jihad exemplified the three sources of Islamic Somali resentment — the antagonism against lax Muslims, the continuing aggression of the Ethiopian state, and the onset of colonialism. Accordingly, he was ecumenical in his targets and attacked the British, French, Italians, and Ethiopians. He was a founder of a religious association/community or jama'a but downplayed other communal organizations such as the clans (it should be noted that these communities consisting of the leaders/shaykh whose members are called dervishes were a a combination of agricultural and religious communities). His contradictory aims included both purifying and attacking Muslims. He did call for one Islamic state. This was to be accomplished by overcoming clan divisions. However, he did this by attacking them. He was an inspiration, but at the same

64 Norman C. Rothman

time his rebellion was devastating to life and property at the cost of perhaps one third of the population of north Somalia.[8]

The balance between the claims of clan and religion has permeated Somali life over the past century. Both the British and Italians did not favor Islamic over clan-related customary law. Often they did not distinguish between the two. Islamic judges could administer both Islamic and customary law. As long as British and Italian laws were not directly contravened, domestic matters such as marriage, divorce, child-support, or in some cases penal cases were handled by the qadis or Islamic judges. Although Sharia was considered useful as in other African colonies with a Muslim or at least nominally Muslim population, in the African colonies, if there was a conflict, colonial decisions were based on the situation on the ground. In Somalia, kin-based (specifically clan and sub-clan) relationships corresponded to communal reality. The Sufi brotherhoods recognized this reality when they routinely asked lineage heads in the sub-clans of the major clans for permission to build their mosques or community/jama'a sites. Indirectly, Islam did benefit as the colonial authorities favored Islamic elites such as the ulama and heads of the waqf (benevolent) foundations who were willing to cooperate and would be appointed to positions of qadis or imams. Although paying lip service to the brotherhoods, the sufi tarikas were either mystical or devotional as were many Quadiriyya or anti-western as were Salihiyya and were not as useful in maintaining law and order as clan leaders.[9]

After independence in 1960, the constitution adopted in 1961 guaranteed freedom of religion but also stated Somalia was an Islamic state. The first two governments proclaimed allegiance to Islamic Socialism which had originally been promoted by Nasser in Egypt where many students had studied in the fifties and sixties (usually at Al-Azhar in Cairo). Islamic Socialism proclaimed that all the components necessary for modernization was to be found in the Muslim scriptures. The first two governments after independence pledged allegiance to this concept.[10]

In October 1969, a leftist radical group seized power and its leader, Siad Barre, and the other members of the Supreme Revolutionary Council proclaimed allegiance to Islamic Socialism initially and even entered the Arab League in 1974 (but soon proclaimed themselves as Marxist scientific socialists as opposed to Islamic socialists). The SRC said that Islamic Socialism was the tool of capitalism and neo-colonization while Scientific Socialism represented the values of "true" Islam. Therefore, religious figures should not be involved in secular affairs. By the late 1970's, religious leaders were being persecuted and religious tribunals were accused of corruption and

Somalia   65

incompetence. In the late 1980's, Barre, who had been a client of the Soviet Union, switched sides to gain assistance so as to gain control over the Ogaden territory which was inhabited by ethnic Somalis against Ethiopia also under a Marxist regime at that time. The attack failed and the money given to Barre by the US was used against his enemies of the Darood clan. Earlier he had arracked the northern Darood religious area of Majeerteen.[11] In general although the strife that engulfed Somalia after 1991-1992 was partly a result of internecine warfare among the clans especially the three largest of Hawiye, Darood, and Isaaq, it was also the result of more militant Islam which reacted against the perceived suppression of Muslims especially after 1980.[12]

Two other factors were the influence of external support and the struggle for dominance in urban areas. The Saudis and other Gulf states opened schools which propagated Wahhabi and Salafi ideas of militant Islam so that a younger generation emerged with more fundamentalist views. Previously, the Somali were either pietistic or against western ideas. This younger group saw Islam as a means of purifying corrupt society.[13] The urban centers especially Mogadishu were also a no man's land between contending clans as they were not traditionally part of the pastoral-agricultural clans. There were additional clans in the mix before the four previously mentioned. In additionally, there were rival sub-clans within the larger clan in the struggle. As time went on, they increasingly invoked Islam to gain support. The tragic incident of Black Hawk down which cost 18 American lives arose out of a feud between Hawiye sub-clans — the Habir Gedir and the Abgaal for control of the city.[14]

When the Barre regime fell in 1990-1991, Somalia gradually lapsed into 3 states; the bulk of south and south-central Somalia currently contested by Hawiye sub-clans and the terrorist organization of Al-Shabaab; north-central-Somalia now the autonomous Puntland — the coast of which is the site of most of Somali piracy, and is controlled by a Darood faction; and the Isaaq-controlled secessionist Somaliland. The turmoil in Somalia started as clan-based warfare (the Hawiye and Isaaq against the Darood government of Barre). However, Islam has become a central part of this struggle. The first Islamic group, the Al Ithiad AL Islamiyam, (AIAI) appeared in a refugee camp outside of Kismayo in 1991-2. It had been formed in the 1980's but gained support for its militancy. It had faded by 2005, but it gave birth to other militant organizations.[15] Subsequent attempts to form a national government foundered on clan rivalry. There was also tension between Islamist groups backed by Arab states and anti-Islamist groups backed by Ethiopia. Even though the early Islamic group, the AIAI, had failed, political Islam still enjoyed great financial support from Saudi Arabia and other Gulf States as well as support from the global Somali diaspora, and training by militants overseas.[16]

The next Islamic militant movement that emerged was the Islamic Courts Union (ICU) that dominated much of central and southern Somalia between mid-2005 and late 2006. The Islamic courts had been a feature of Somali society for decades. In 2003, they united and were supported by the business community who were tired of the chaos in Magadishu, Merca, Barawe, and other cities as well as the out of control warlords,. It soon became apparent that it was increasingly influenced by hardline forces. Its military wing, al-Shabaab which had started as the youth faction of AIAI not only announced a jihadist platform but indicated it had irrendentist claims (the national flag has 5 stars that represent North and South Somalia, Djibouti, the Ogadan region of Ethiopia, and the Northeast Province of Kenya). At end of 2006, Somalia's historic enemy, Ethiopia, sent in troops that ousted the ICU from the capital. While the nominal central government remains ineffective, many Somalis have come to rely on their traditional support in the clans.[17]

Since 2007, portions of southern Somalia have been under Al-Shabaab control. Reportedly, it receives financial and logistical support from Al-Qaeda and other radical groups. As late as 2011, it generated 70-100 million dollars a year from taxing the areas it controls. Its activities plus years of lawlessness helped engender a famine in southern Somalia in recent years that cost an estimated 250,000 lives half of whom were children under 5.[18]

Al-Shabaab has links not only with Al-Qaeda but also such other extremist organizations as AQIM (Al-Qaeda in the Maghrib) and Boko Haram. It has attacked and been attacked by both Ethiopia and Kenya. Its latest attack in Kenya was its attack on a Nairobi shopping center which cost 68 lives in September 2013. In 2012, it attacked the capital city of Addis Ababa with specific onslaughts on the President's Office and the headquarters of the African Union. Recently, it demonstrated its continued strength by an attack on the Presidential Palace in Mogadishu.[19]

Al-Shabaab is now an outlaw organization. The United Nations has sent in troops to the capital and some semblance of order has been established. The government has a new president, Sheik Mohammad (elected in September 2012),[20] who is trying to extend control at least as far as central Somalia goes. A rival party in the hinterland has emerged, the Party of Islam, which may diminish its influence. In the meantime, Al-Shabaab can still bring 7,000 to 10,000 men into the field and appears to have some support from Eritrea which has ongoing disputes with Ethiopia. Attempts by forces like the Navy

Seals in October 2013 have still not succeeded in taking out the command center.[21]

Somalis have grown tired of the turmoil and would like to return to the days when the clans and the brotherhoods defined their lives and religion. However, it was these very clans, and, to some extent, the brotherhoods, that promoted a decentralized and fragmented Somalia. It is this heritage which forms the background of the tragic situation today.

Chapter 7

TANZANIA

The history of Islam in Tanzania can be divided into three parts: The Swahili phase before 1800; the Zanzibar-Oman phase in the 19th century and the colonial and national phase.

The Swahili people of East Africa were traders on a global scale. At one time or another, they were key players in the commerce and the economy of the Mediterranean, Europe, and Asia. Ethnically, the ancestors of the Swahili were the Bantu farmers who used iron hoes and iron spears and reached the coast between 100 B.C. and 700 A.D. Both the language and ethnic composition of this group are basically African with admixtures from groups who came from the Indian Ocean — mostly Arabs, but also Persians, Indians, and Malays. Even today, the Swahili people, who are mostly located in coastal cities such as Mombasa, Dar es Salaam, Kilwa, and Zanzibar, have retained a cultural distinctiveness, with a separate written language using both Arabic and Latin characters in different scripts, a separate artistic tradition, and such separate artifacts as illustrated Korans, distinctive jewelry, indigenous building motifs, group-derived musical instruments, and even a distinct tradition of wood-carving. Often they are recognized through their dress, as the men often wore white gowns and the women wore black robes. Devout Muslims, they often send their young men to mosque schools. The Indian Ocean as seen by the main participants in the African aspect of the Indian Ocean (Muslims and South India) was one continuum which extended from the Red Sea and eastern Mediterranean all the way to the Straits of Malacca and to the Indonesian archipelago as far as the present island of Sunda. The emphasis of both Muslims and Indians in Africa was the East Coast, which was not only part of the Indian Ocean littoral, but historically was part of Islam.[1]

Islam was unifying element in much of the Indian Ocean, especially on both sides — the east African coast and the Malay world. The east African societies relied on Islam to help create their world since their identity derived not only from commercial links with co-religionists but on specific modes of social and commercial behavior. The Muslim religion gave prescriptions as to everyday conduct. The Koran had specific admonitions on fair practice in the market place. The Koranic injunction to have balance scales led to the appearance of a market inspector called the muhtash whose specific job was to oversee local transactions and check weights and measures among other duties. Muslims send their young men to mosque schools. As is the custom, they tended to practice traditional occupations such as shopkeeping and trading.. There was a hierarchy of custom rates ranging from 2.5% for believers to 5% for "protected" non-believers to 10% for other non-believers.[2]

In general, the influence of Islam not only as a religion but as a way of life thoroughly permeated Swahili culture. In addition to literacy in Swahili based on Arabic script, literacy in Arabic was a sign of culture and upper class. By the fourteenth century, the mosques were the most important building in town and in many places they became the dividing line between patricians and commoners. They exhibited typically Muslim features such as muhrabs and kubilu as well as the ubiquitous minarets. They faced in the direction of Mecca and Medina. (Parenthetically, it is interesting to note that Islamic tombs were often decorated with Chinese porcelain) and the Swahili language shows foreign influence such as muhindi (Hindi for wheat).[3]

Dress also reflected external influence. The elite wore Muslim ceremonial clothing on special days and in public. The costume would include such traditional items as the long white robe, a turban, a sword and dagger, and sandals made of animal hide. In contrast, commoners were forbidden to wear ceremonial robes or religious footwear, or even to carry ceremonial weapons such as the sword and dagger in public.[4]

Most visually, architecture and social space tended to mirror the Muslim world. Their stone houses exhibited features associated with Islamic house motifs as arches and niches. Not only did the mosque divide many towns into upper and lower sections, but the architecture reflected ritual influenced habitations. In addition to the mosques and tombs, the grandest buildings were the great palaces which combined living quarters and governmental functions modeled on Baghdad and Cairo. The grandest building was the sultan's palace in Kilwa which was over an acre in size and contained more than a hundred rooms in the Muslim style. In contrast, the quarters of the commoners in most Swahili cities were small and built from coral and sun-dried clay sometimes with a lime overlay. Conversely, the houses of the upper classes were similar (but not identical as Swahili architecture has distinctive elements) to that of wealthy families of the Middle East as they were often multi-storied with a front portico and an inner courtyard. Unlike the one or two room clay and coral structures, there were private rooms as opposed to public rooms specifically preserved for the families and households. In all, the differentiated status in various aspects of life was meant to convey a "special" external origin which in this case derived from cultures predominantly but not exclusively Muslim which had come through the Indian Ocean.[5]

The central part of the Swahili Coast was called Zanj and its southern part corresponds to present-day coastal Tanzania. The major towns in this area were also located on islands off the coast — Zanzibar, Pemba, and Mafia. However, the most important town at this time was the island city of Kilwa which was to dominate the gold trade from the state of Zimbabwe and its successors in south central Africa between the twelfth and fifteenth centuries. Today, Kilwa is in southern Tanzania, but it was considered one of the great cities of the world before 1500. Trade was mainly in gold, iron, ivory, and other animal products of the African interior for beads, textiles, jewelry, porcelain, and spices from Asia.[6]

By the 12th century, under the rule of the Abu'-Mawahib dynasty, Kilwa had become the most powerful city on the East African coast. At the zenith of its power in the 15th century, the Kilwa Sultanate claimed authority over the city-states of Malindi, Mvita (Mombasa), Pemba Island, Zanzibar, Mafia Island, Grande Comore, Sofala, and the trading posts across the channel on Madagascar. It had its own factories for weaving textiles from silk and also the use of kilns and iron works to export a variety of goods such as clothing and utensils which could be sold in the interior of Africa or overseas. Kilwa became famous for its Friday mosque which because of its great wealth was considered the finest in all of East Africa. Even today, the tombs that were erected as well as the Sultan's palace are considered prime examples of Islamic architecture.[7]

The cities of Zanj had literacy based on Arabic, but by 1500 had a separate written language based on Arabic letters literacy in both was considered a mark of culture. The Swahili culture was mainly Sunni Muslim, and it followed the law code prominent in its closest neighbors (Yemen and Hadhramaut) — the Shafi'i law code.[8]

After 1500 as Portuguese and Arabs fought for control, the fortunes of these city-states on the East coast of Africa including those on the Zanj coast declined although they would have brief periods of revival. However, during this time, Islam was confined to the coast and its immediate hinterland. This would change after 1800. By the beginning of the 19th century, much of the East African coast from Mombasa to Kilwa was under Omani control. By 1840, the Sultan of Oman had moved his capital from Muscat to Zanzibar. This move was in response to a plantation culture which had grown up in Zanzibar and its sister island of Pemba, These plantations of cloves and cinnamon were labor intensive and required slaves (permitted in the Qur'an). To feed the slaves, grain growing areas were established on the hinterland. This traffic in slaves became the largest in the world and continued until abolition in 1890. As further plantations were developed on the mainland, the slave trade grew until it encompassed much of East and East Central Africa. Much of this traffic was carried out by Muslim traders with African affiliates. Greater inland contact eventually led to greater conversion in the decades after 1840.[9]

Conversion in the hinterland not only came through the arrival of Muslim traders but through the return of Africans who had been to the coast and had returned to their home villages with their new religion. The end of plantation slavery after 1890 also led to the return of former slaves who also brought Islam with them.[10]

As the century wore on, markets were established in the interior which led to trade routes along which came Muslim traders who brought their religion with them. Two of the major trade routes ran from Dar-es-Salaam (literally heart of Islam) which had been founded in the mid-19th century to Lake Tanganyika along which ivory and later slaves were traded. They ran then towns such as Ugogo and Tabora and were conducted in cooperation with local peoples especially the Nyamwezi. These routes and the trade that was conduct as well as the peoples engaged in this trade became agents of islamization.[11]

The islamization process continued under the colonial period first under the Germans between 1885 and 1915; then under the British until 1963. The military conquest of what was to become Tanganyika was carried out to some extent with African auxiliaries who had become converted to Islam. Theses soldiers were then stationed in the administrative centers that were established first by the Germans and then by the British. Often, they would retire in the areas in which they were settled.[12]

Muslims benefitted from two other factors during the colonial era. Often, they were the beneficiaries of patronages as they were appointed chiefs, clerks, and tax collectors where they came into contact with and could influence the local population.[13] They were also a unifying factor in a territory with over

100 separate ethnic groups, After WWI, Christian missionaries and education centers began to catch up but the Muslims were there first.[14]

Some traditional trading towns were centers of influence in their respective areas especially those towns along the pre-colonial Indian Ocean-Lake Tanganyika route. They often became administrative centers. These towns tended to mirror aspects of Swahili culture (a Sunni, Shafi'i school of law, dress, food, etc.). Swahili as the universal trading language and "lingua franca" was particularly influential in this respect.[15]

Even before Independence, Islam gained credence as a symbol of proto-nationalism. In some degree, it was based on the rural followers of the Quadariyya order. It also included members of the major Ngoni tribe which was becoming Islamized at the time. It did, however, gain support from some non-Muslim elements of the population in southern Tanganyika.[16]

After WWI and especially after WWII, political organizations had Muslim support. Early associations such as the Tanganyika African Association (TAA) had Muslim supporters among Islamic urban population such as teachers and clerks. It was replaced by the Tanganyika African National Union (TANU) which was also supported by and contained Muslims.[17]

In the late colonial and early national period, as was the case in some other emerging African nations, newly emerging African leaders wanted to deemphasize traditional factors. In Tanganyika (soon to be Tanzania), the newly formed TANU was led by Julius Nyerere who wanted to avoid excessive influence of religious. Following this policy and the national emphasis on ujamaa (national community hood) (annunciated in his Arusha declaration shortly after independence), Nyerere chose to place nation-wide values above any sectarian identity. As Zanzibar had just become affiliated with Tanganyika (in 1964) after its African majority had overthrown the Arab-based Omani dynasty which looked to the Middle East, and by inference, Islam and was for a number of years Marxist, Nyerere wanted to emphasize nationhood. Although TANU had Muslim supporters, some Muslims felt that it was insufficient and formed the All-Muslim National Union of Tanganyika (AMNUT) to lobby for more educational and and patronage jobs for Muslim. Its counterpart during the early national period, Dawa al-Islamiyya, argued for much of the same thing. The leaders of both movements met opposition from TANU and were either expelled from the party or placed in detention.[18]

In general, the ruling party, TANU or its successor CCM displayed a preference at least originally for pro-government Islamists of a Swahili background from the islands or coast. In 1969, the government in its desire to appear above all special interests nationalized all primary schools. A number of Muslims were still aggrieved as it appeared that ujamaa or social development through education was not being achieved as it still had the appearance of a preference for Christians over Muslims. The approximately equal percentages of Muslims and Christians which has resulted in a rotation between Christians and Muslims since Nyerere left the presidency in 1987 has not reduced tensions between the two groups or between Muslims and the government. The fate of the venerable East African Welfare Society (EAMWS) illustrates this underlying tension. It was both pan-Islamist and non-sectarian when a dispute broke out, between pan-Islamists and pro-government factions, the movement was banned and replaced by a pro-government Council for Muslims, Bakwata. Another organization, Warsha, which supports young Muslim writers and produced textbooks for the seminaries captured the imagination of young Muslims, was considered a threat and licked out of Bakwata. It continues to thrive.[19]

As the one-party situation has given way to a multi-party situation in post-Nyerere Tanzania (although strictly sectarian parties are forbidden); Muslim-oriented political movements have come to the fore.[20] They are often supported financially by Muslim embassies that finance new mosques, new schools, scholarships. These organizations include the Muslim Preachers Union, the Muslim Student Association, the Union of Muslim youths, the Islamic Propagation Center, and the Council of Muslim/Islamic Teachers. They are influenced by Warsha, which continues to write extensively, encourage scholarship, and even taken to circulating letters and writings at Friday prayers at mosques. It is particularly appealing to young people as it both aims to correct abuses in the existing social order while working for an idealized Islamic social order. Its standing is such that some Muslims see it as an alternate to the ulama.[21]

Zanzibar is more of a fit for radical Islam. It has been in a union with Tanganyika since 1964 and has a semi-autonomous status. As part of Tanzania, although it has only million of Tanzania's 45 million it is quite influential as it gave the united Tanzania its second president after Nyerere retired.[22] Historically, it had been independent for a millennium before the sultan moved his headquarters there between 1832 and 1840. Thereafter, Zanzibar controlled a vast empire including much of what today is Tanzania, Kenya, and Malawi before becoming a protectorate of Britain between 1890 and 1963. Zanzibar then underwent a revolution where it overthrew the sultan and came under the control of its African majority. For a few years, it followed a nationalist/leftist path in reaction to the Arab/Muslim orientation of the previous regime, but since 1971-72, it has returned to a more Islamic approach.[23]

Except for the 7/8 year interlude, Zanzibar has had a strong history of Islamic nationalism. There were, in fact, two schools of thought. One group maintained that nationalism was incompatible with Islam as it promoted one single group while Islam was universal. The other group maintained that nationalism and patriotism were compatible with Islam. After WWII, the Young Men's Muslim Association which had been founded to promote education among young men pressed for more rights and social reform. Between 1945 and 1963, Muslim feeling was divided between the party representing the nearly three quarter African majority on the islands of Zanzibar and Pemba (which with the island city of Mafia and a few outlets compose the archipelago) (the Afro-Shirazi party) and the ZNP which represented the Arab/South Asian minority). After questionable election results, the latter was installed. A month later, it was overthrown on a violent coup which took 20,000 lives mostly from the Arab and South Asian minorities.[24] Since the 1970's, Muslims have complained of neglect in favor of the "mainland" although Zanibari politicians are included in the Tanzanian leadership. They are concerned with what it feels are unfavorable economic prospects, and favoritism to Christians in higher education (concerns also shared by young Muslims on the "mainland"). As a result, Muslims have begun to organize with aid from Muslim countries abroad and the oppority afforded by the relative openness of the system since the multi-party arrangement was introduced in 1992.[25] However, radical Islamic groups have found outlets. In the 1980"s, an organization in Pemba arose, Bismullah, which demanded the end of the union and a return to a more ideal Islamic society.[26]

Afterward somewhat more moderate associations have become more prominent. The Daresalaam University Muslim Trusteeship promotes education for Muslims at the university levels while other associations want separate secondary education. The efforts have paid off as a separate Muslim Academy has opened which caters to Islamic students. Moreover secondary education is available in English, Kiswahili, and Arabic. Also young Muslim scholars have studied abroad.[27] The current radical movement, Uamsho or "Awakening" is demanding the secession of Zanzibar from the Tanzanian mainland. They have waged violent demonstrations in spite of a ban. The new policy which now allows proportional representation in the government instead of "winner take all" so far has not met their grievances.[28]

Currently, violent transnational Islamic groups such as al-Shabaab and Al-Qaeda in East Africa (AQEA) are not prominent threats. However, transnational terrorist attacks from Islamic extremists can happen as exemplified by the attacks on the American embassy in Dar-es-Salaam (and Nairobi) in 1998. It should be noted that there is a wide variety of Islamic expression including Sufi brotherhoods. Although the bulk of the population is Sunni and many of the upper and middle class follow the mainstream Hanafi law code, much of the rest of the population follow the Shafi'i tradition and a few who have been influenced by Omani and Yemeni culture who are usually non-African follow Maliki and Hanbali legal traditions. Zanzibar with a stronger Omani connection had offshoots of Kharijism such as Ibaddiya and of Shiite influences such as the Ismaili and Bohra beliefs, but the latter have few followers who are almost entirely Asian. There have been violent attacks in recent years on both Muslim and Christian buildings so sectarianism is an issue.[29]

Muslim discontent is based on domestic grievances rather than an international desire for a universal caliphate. These days, Muslim identity especially on the Tanzanian mainland is expressed in mosque attendance and in the wearing of Islamic garb.[30] In general, Tanzania with over 100 ethnic/linguistic groups as well as two separate but not necessarily equal groups has a difficulty balancing act. So far, it has achieved a balance. but overall equilibrium remains precarious.

PART V: CAUCASUS

As was indicated in the introduction, Islam has been present in Europe almost from the beginning with Muslims being present in Iberia since the 8th century, Italy since before the 9th century, Russia proper since the 13th century, and the Balkans in the 14th century. Today, they are the fastest-growing group in Europe. In nowhere, however, has Islam, been planted so long and so prominently then the Caucasus. This is most obvious in the Southern Caucasus occupied in the southwest by Azerbaijan.

Chapter 8

AZERBAIJAN: BETWEEN ASIA AND EUROPE

Azerbaijan is in the southern part of the Caucasus right across from its Turkic kinsmen on the eastern side of the Caspian Sea which borders Azerbaijan. Technically, it straddles the border between Asia and Europe. The policy of the government has been to identify with Europe by seeking admission to the European Union and strengthening its contacts with the West.[1]

At the same time, Azerbaijan is located between the Caspian and Black Seas. Historically, the area has been the turnstile for maritime traffic of the Black and Caspian Seas, with connections to the Great Silk Road. More significantly, it has been the land bridge for both north-south and south-north migrations and invasions. After 2000 B.C.E, people from Central Asia and the steppes north of the Caucasus Mountains invaded the ancient Near East and established the Hittite and the Assyrian empires in central Anatolia and northern Mesopotamia respectively. After 800 C.E./A.D., Turkic speakers mostly the Oghuz confederation used the area as an invasion route into the Middle East. Invasion also came from the opposite direction. Persian speakers invaded the area several times between 600 B.C.E. and 600 C.E. Islam was also brought from the south by Arabs in the late 7th century. Both Alexander the Great and the Roman Empire included the area in their empires.

In the process, Azerbaijan has undergone several identity changes which underline its border status. Its Christianity dates from 100 A.D./C.E. while its nominal overlord, the Roman Empire, was still pagan. The Persian interlude introduced Zorastrianism into the country and remnants of both still exist. Islam dates from 650 while the country has been preeminently Shiite since 1500. The ancient inhabitants were called Albanians whose ethnicity has not been established. The ethnic identity changed after the Turkic invasion in the 9th and 10th centuries. Today, a Turkic dialect most closely identified with Turkmenistan and Turkey is spoken.[2]

Currently, most Azeris consider themselves as part of the Turkic family. Others maintain that they are related to Persian speakers who have been Turkified.[3] A similar process occurred in Bulgaria where the Bulgars who were originally a Turkic group became Slavicized through language and religion.

The country is pulled in several directions. It is geographically between Europe and Asia. Its neighbors to the west — Georgia and Armenia are Orthodox Christian (although Azerbaijan has had a century-old dispute with the latter most recently over the border area of Nagorno-Karabakh), but Iran and Turkey to the southeast and southwest are Muslim. Also since 1828, the country has been divided with present-day Azerbaijan having a population of 8 million while 18 million to the south are now part of Iran where they constitute nearly one/quarter of the population second only to the Farsi-speaking Persians.[4]

Typical of a border state, Islam has not been a predominant factor for the non-Iranian portion of the Azeri figure unlike their Iranian kinsmen. Rather, their identity has been more with traditional Turkic culture than with Islam. Islam is considered part of the national identity but does not define it. In addition, the multi-confessional heritage of the country plus decades of atheistic Soviet rule which furthered dampened religious zeal has tended not to support widespread fundamentalist feeling (although since the breakup of the Soviet Union, there has been a fundamentalist party, the Islamist Party of Azerbaijan).[5]

Azerbaijan commingles religion with custom. Despite a population that is 93% Muslim, the Azeri constitution permits every faith to practice religion. These include Russian and Armenian orthodox Christians as well as pockets of Judaism and Zorastrianism.[6]

The Muslim population is divided into about 60+% Shia and the remaining Sunni. The Sunni appear to be increasing in population. Currently, the Shia predominate in the south and the Sunni are predominant in the north. The south is influenced by Iran across the border while the north is influenced by Sunni Turkey. Cognizant of this division, the administrative Muslim Spiritual Board of the Transcaucasus headquartered in Baku divides its leadership. Its chairman is Shia while the deputy is Sunni.[7]

In general, fervor is relatively low. Less than one/tenth of Azeri people consider themselves to be devoted Muslims. In part, this was a heritage from

Azerbaijan: Between Asia and Europe 81

Soviet times. Unlike their co-religionists, the Azeri did not find ways to practice their religion clandestinely. As an example of this, Azeri Shia celebrates Ashura, the most holy day of the Shia calendar which centers on the martyrdom of Hussein in 680. Devout Muslims stress the religious connotations while others including most Shia see Islam as part of folklore and Ashura as a symbol for survival against overwhelming odds — a thinly veiled analogy to Soviet times when religion was repressed.[8]

Islam has staged a comeback when one considers its state at the end of the 1980's. At that time, there were fewer than 70 mullahs. There were so few clerics that a mullah would often perform both Sunni and Shia ceremonies. Since independence in 1991, both Iran and Turkey have sent missionaries which aided in a revival of Islam.[9]

Soon, however, the missionaries overplayed their hand. The Islamic Party of Azerbaijan openly followed the lead of its benefactor, Iran, and advocated the establishment of an Islamic republic. The Azeri authorities soon became suspicious that the party was spying for Iran and outlawed it. Since then, all missionaries must register with the Spiritual Board in order to visit local communities. In addition, the number of missionaries and the length of their stay are now limited.[10]

Fundamentalism has not been very successful in Azerbaijan due to the tradition of relative tolerance based on pluralism. For two thousand years, it had a thriving Jewish community in its midst while, until recently, it had good relations with Orthodox Christians. The fight over Nagorno-Karabakh (an Armenian enclave within Azerbaijan) which has been invaded and occupied by the Armenians did cause outbreaks in Baku, the capital of Azerbaijan.. These attacks were directed against Armenians as a group rather their religion.[11]

Pan-Islamism has had to contend with Pan-Turkism. The latter seeks to unify Turkic or Turkic-speaking peoples from Central Asia, Turkey, and Azerbaijan. Pan-Islamism was represented early in the twentieth century by the Musavat Party which advocated Muslim unity and independence. The outbreak of the Bolshevik Revolution led to much bloodshed and ultimately its suppression in 1920 after brief independence between 1918 and 1920. The Soviets sought to eradicate all sources of nationalism and replaced the Arabic alphabet first with the Latin alphabet (1924) and then with the Cyrillic alphabet (1940). After independence, Latin was reintroduced.[12]

Azeri sentiments are similar to Central Asia in the tying of religion to culture or in some cases pre-Islamic customs. As an example, one can point to the favorite Azeri holiday of Novruz which has been celebrated for nearly

3000 thousand years and is celebrated in connection with vernal equinox on March 21. It is rooted in the Zorastrian religion and is a heritage of Persian culture when their relatives the Medes started to filter into the area in the first millennium B.C.E. Although Ramadan is observed, Novruz or "new birth' is far more popular.[13]

Today, Islam rather than Islamic fundamentalism is more prevalent. Even though Azerbaijan borders Iran which has two thirds of the ethnic Azeri population and is the epitome of Shiite fundamentalism, and the country has engaged with Christian Armenia in a long running dispute, Azerbaijan has steered a middle course. This is particularly impressive as it borders the Caucasus Mountains on the south. This volatile region has seen Muslim-inspired uprisings against Russia and Christian/Muslim communal strife in Dagestan, Chechyna, and Ingushtiya. Neighboring Christian Orthodox Georgia has had Muslim revolts in the province of Abhazia (South Ossetia's struggle was ethnic).[14]

Given these factors, there has been very little violence arising from religion in the country. Outwardly, Islam has blossomed in the republic after independence as new mosques and new madrasahs were built. Young Azeri travelled overseas to Islamic institutions of higher learning in Iran, Turkey, Saudi Arabia, Egypt, and Pakistan. Azeri leaders have routinely gone on religious pilgrimages. Yet, in spite of these manifestations of religious feelings, in a recent survey, only 17.7% of respondents indicated that they observed the Muslim injunction of Daily Prayer.[15]

The relationship between government and Islam has undergone different phases in the post-independence period. In the initial phase, secular nationalists and observant Muslims had cooperated in the struggle for Independence. At this stage, political parties who identified themselves contented themselves with the maintenance of Islam as a strictly ethical and religious element in social life not political life. During this period, the Law of Freedom of Religion was adopted. All religious property that had been taken during the Soviet era was restored. The Spiritual Department was separated from the state and all state assistance to the department was ended. All clergy were henceforth to be paid by public donations. Freedom of worship was inaugurated.[16]

The second phase came with the present regime. It was anxious to gain legitimacy so that the new president, Heydar Aliyev, swore fidelity to both Constitution and the Qur'an. In return, the supposedly independent Spiritual Department now began to give all government actions its stamp of approval and devoted itself to propaganda on behalf of his government. His son and successor who took over after his death in October 2003 has continued his policies.[17]

The attitude toward other forms of religion is quite different. The radicalism of the Islamic Party of Azerbaijan as well as the radicalism of certain missionaries led, as we have seen, to the outlawing of the first and the limiting of the other. However, alternates to "official Islam" continue to be active. Wahhabi/Salafi missionary activity has continued. The Salafis in particular have been active and by 2003 had 65 mosques in the country).[18] By 2006, membership in Wahhabi/Salafi organizations was over 25,000. Overall, through the efforts of these groups and government support, mosques had increased from fewer than 70 to 1400 in two decades.[19] Nevertheless, although the Wahhabi/Salafi groups have not been proscribed, they are subject to arrest. Other radical fundamentalist organizations such as Hizbollah are closely monitored. Unlike official Islam, these organizations are anti-Turkic, anti-Semitic, and anti-American. They look on religion as nationalism as "shirk" or anti-Islamic and a violation of monotheism.[20]

In spite of the above and the continued activity of radical missionaries especially from Saudi Arabia and Iran, Islam remains rather shallow as public knowledge about basic rituals continues to be rather limited. Syncretism with Turkic customs and pre-Islamic religions continues unabated. Fortunetellers use the Qur'an, for instance, to foretell the future. Many Shia believe the 10th day of Muharram (a holiday which involves whipping and self-flagellation) is the most important ceremony in Islam (ignoring Eid and Ashura) since they do not pray or follow basic precepts of Islam. Often lines for basic rituals (funerals and marriages) are not recited as some mullahs still do know them.[21]

Most Azeri continue to view Islam as part of their national identity. They also continue to reject the mixture of religion and politics propagated by religious radicals. Islam is a national characteristic just as the Turkic language and culture are. Accordingly, no single group can claim a special status.[22]

So indifferent are Azeri to the performance of Islamic duties that, Azerbaijan, alone among Islamic countries, does not fill the quota allotted to countries to make the pilgrimage to Mecca. Instead, vacant places are sold to pilgrims from Chechnya and Dagestan. Many Azeri also reject the wearing of garments that signify religion.[23]

Azerbaijan is a moderate secular country. Nevertheless, sectarian differences can lead to tension. The Iranian influence on Shiites in the south is counterbalanced by Salafist (mostly from Egypt) in the north among Sunni. Although the country as whole is not zealous when it comes to religion, fundamentalist groups such as the Salafists can be appealing as they preach a universal message that transcends sects. They also benefit from discontent with the government whose leadership is considered both autocratic and corrupt by many Azeri. In this respect, not much of the country's wealth in oil and gas has as yet filtered down to the masses.[24]

External events have increased dissatisfaction with the government. The presence of coreligionists such as Chechens has increased ill-feeling. Furthermore, the Armenian conquest of Nagorno-Karabahk had led to several hundred thousand refugees in Azerbaijan. This event was attributed to governmental incompetence. The feeling that official Islam is an arm of government has further embittered the population.[25]

Overall, there is a feeling that there has been a general decline in morality and ethics. Newly-arrived Islamists and fundamentalists therefore find a ready audience. In addition, young Azeri educated abroad have been exposed to radical ideas-both fundamentalist and Islamist. They bring these ideas back with them when they return to Azerbaijan. If these trends continue, the general secular orientation of Azerbaijan may alter.

On the whole, however, although Islam was introduced to what is now Azerbaijan as early as the 7th century and the bulk of its kinsmen live next door in Iran, Azerbaijan has tended to align with Europe. It belongs to the Council of Europe, Office of Cooperation and Security in Europe, and is an associate of the Nato Partnership for Peace. It is an associate of the European Union and may one day seek full membership. Economically with large oil and gas deposits, it has ties with European consumers with a new pipeline which bypasses Russia. The Royal Dutch Shell Company and the state energy company are jointly involved in the exploration of new energy resources.[26]

Overall, Azerbaijan follows a secular policy similar to the church and state policies of Europe. It does not go by Sharia law. It prohibits religious leaders from serving in public office while holding a religious office. Religious entities are registered and cannot engage in politics as organizations.[27]

Its foreign and domestic policy is moderate. It is wary about Wahabbism even though Saudi Arabia supports religious activities and its relationship with Iran is poor due to the latter country's support of Armenia during the dispute over Nagorno-Karabakh as well as the position of the very large Azeri minority in Iran. It is the only Muslim state near the Middle East to have a close and strong (and public) relationship with Israel. Domestically, it has a Freedom of Religion Law. Article 6 of this law indicates that the educational system should be separate from religion.[28]

Azerbaijan may not quite meet the European criteria on totally free and fair elections, but it has a relatively good record on human rights. Although most Russians and Armenians have departed, there have not been avowedly anti-Christian riots as opposed to anti-Armenian and anti-Russian demonstrations. There is no anti-Semitism in Azerbaijan (Jews have lived in the country since 400 B.C.) and today there are still three separate synagogues in the capital of Baku. The Baha'i sect is persecuted in Iran but has received official recognition in Azerbaijan.[29] Overall, Azerbaijan has gone its own way when other countries such as Turkey (at least under Erdogan) appear to be more receptive to Islamic fundamentalism. In spite of ethnic and religious affiliation, the country is a model for secularism in an Islamic state. It has its problems with corruption with the temptation of oil and gas discoveries and the political system remains somewhat authoritarian, but it seems at the moment to have found a balance between church and state.

Chapter 9

DAGESTAN

Islam had a much slower process of adoption in the North Caucasus than in the South Caucasus due to the diversity of people as well as topography. It has taken a millennium for its inculcation. Nowhere is this more obvious than in Dagestan. It is the Russian Republic with a Muslim majority that contains the largest number of Muslims. Within this figure, however, there are 41 recognized nationalities. The largest of these, the Avars, constitute just 29 % of the population. Within this group, there are 15 distinct ethno-linguistic subdivisions.[1] The second largest group, the Dargins, constitute 16.5% of the population but also have three subdivisions. Overall, there were 41 recognized ethno-linguistic nationalities in the last census.[2]

Topography has also played a role. As part of the northern Caucasus, Dagestan is a land of rolling hills, plateaus, and mountains. This has been an impediment to outsiders whether peaceful or military. Often, Islamic missionaries could most conveniently reach the country via the east, the Caspian Sea, or north from Azerbaijan. As a result, although Islam purportedly entered the country as early as 642, the bulk of the population did not embrace Islam until 1500 with some holdouts until 1800.[3]

Traditionally, Sufism was the dominant force in Dagestani Islam although most Dagestani (as well as other north Caucasion Muslims) are Sunni who follow the Shafi'i law code. It was really not until after 1000 that Islam made major inroads as Sufism did not reach its full development until that time. Its mystical devotional focus fit in very well with local Dagestani culture. The most active Sufi orders were the Quadiriyya and the Naqshbandi orders who were most active in the 11th and 15th century respectively. They established tariqas or brotherhoods throughout the country. These brotherhoods were headed by a sheikh with disciples called murids. The stress on devotional aspects of religion rather than in texts in Arabic or Persian which many people could not read appealed to the average Dagestani.[4]

Both Sufism and the Sunni code brought a sense of order and solidary to the disparate population. Sufism allowed all groups to connect with traditional identification with ancestors or the spiritual world as a form of syncretism. Sunni brought Dagestan into contact with a law code, a political philosophy, and a general jurisprudence which gave order and political structure to their existence.[5]

In the early to mid-nineteenth century, Russian expansion into the Caucasus provoked resistance in Dagestan and its neighbor to the southwest, Chechnya. The opposition was Islamic in form and was called the murid movement. It was based on the local tarika or brotherhoods, and took its name from the followers of the local teacher in the brotherhood or sheikh/shaykh. They were led by a charismatic leader, Imam Shamil, and it lasted from 1831 to 1859 before it was suppressed.[6] Shamil's resistance derived from the naqshabandi order and was based on the concept of gazavat or "liberation" based on Islamic teaching. This jihad was not only waged against Russian colonialism but against traditional social structures which were deemed to be un-Islamic. As a consequence, the Russians supported traditional values and customs (adat) and used them against Sufi orders.[7]

Continuing Islamic feeling was manifested by Dagestani (as well as Chechen and other Caucasian Muslims) anger against the Russian attack on the Ottoman Empire in 1877-78 followed by other developments, Feelings were aroused by the attempted introduction of the Cyrillic alphabet in place of Arabic in 1912-14. It was later rescinded. WWI also aroused pan-Islamic feels when Russia opposed Turkey and fighting took place in the Caucasus.[8]

The coming of the Bolshevik Revolution coincided with a period of growth for Islam. There was a separate Muslim publishing house. There were 2,311 maktabs (equivalent to Koranic schools in the Middle East) as well as 400 madrassas and over 1700 mosques. When the Revolution got underway, Islamic societies proliferated. During the Civil War which ensued, Dagestanis fought with the Bolsheviks as they identified the anti-Bolsheviks with the old tsarist regime. After the Bolshevik Revolution, Dagestan alone of the North Caucasian peoples retained a separate identity.[9]

By September 1920, disappointed by Bolshevik rule, there was an Islamic uprising in the Avar areas. To alleviate discontent, the Soviets made some compromises. They gave lip-service to Sharia as the law of the law. In 1923, sharia district courts were established and were followed by village Sharia courts in 1925. In 1924, the republic recognized Islamic holidays such as Kurban-Bairan and Uraza-Nairan as official holidays. By 1925, there were approximately 40,000 Islamic clergy — a significant part of the population at that time. The number of mosques had grown to over 2,000.[10]

In 1927-28, came a turnabout. Secure in position, the Soviets no longer felt the need to placate Islam in Dagastan. In 1927, district and village sharia courts were abolished and Sharia law disallowed. In 1928, the madrassas and mosques were closed. Soon after, persecution of Muslims began. Muslim clergy were arrested and a number of high dignitaries were exiled and even executed in the late nineteen twenties and early nineteen thirties, Sufi brotherhoods were driven underground in the nineteen thirties.[11]

By 1940, Islamic activities had been suppressed. Islamic practice and education had deteriorated. Islamic activity was driven underground. Some Islamic observance lingered, but it tended to be in somewhat isolated rural villages away from Communist influence. The Sufi orders continued but in an underground fashion.[12]

As the Soviet Union disintegrated, religious feeling revived. Islam in the Caucasus was reinvigorated by the arrival of imams educated at Central Asian madrassas. In September 1990, the Supreme Soviet of the USSR passed a law that permitted religious liberty. There was an immediate response in Dagestan as open observance occurred and Sufi brotherhoods once again operated out in the open, By 1998, there were 1670 mosques and 106 registered religious schools and an Islamic university.[13] Other markers showed the upsurge in Islamic feeling. About 20% of Dagestanis were involved in Islamic education. More than half of the pilgrims making the hajj to Islamic holy places were from Dagestan. There was a surge of support for students to study abroad in Muslim countries in the Middle East and Southeast Asia. Islamic literature flooded into the country.[14]

Since this period, the Islamic situation in Dagestan has been influenced by two factors. The spillover effect from the Chechen conflict has found its echo in neighboring Dagestan. Furthermore, there is the arrival of Salafis and Wahhabis in an area where the somewhat non-fundamentalist Sufi/Sunni brand had previously held sway. The twin effects of these two trends was illustrated by the extremist fundamentalist Islamic incursion into Dagestan that took place between August 2, 1999 and September 16, 1999.[15] This event was the climax of these two trends. It was also exacerbated by economic hard times which had left unemployment and underemployment to a nearly 80% rate particularly in the rural areas.[16] At loose ends, many young men went to fundamentalist training camps led by Chechen Islamist fighters. Chechen

Islamic leader, Basaev, and Saudi Wahhabi fundamentalist, E-al-Khattab, planned this incursion. Early that year (before the Russian reconquest of Chechnya in 2000-2002),[17] Basaev had convened a conference of delegates from Chechnya and Dagestan wherein he proclaimed his goal was to establish an Islamic State in the North Caucasus and that his immediate objective was to raise military forces to conduct operations so as to liberate the territory through a jihad.[18]

Several months later, this declaration was followed by the invasion and the proclamation of an Islamic Republic. This episode retarded rather than advanced the cause as it in the minds of many Dagestanis identified Islamic fundamentalism with terrorism and served as a justification of Russian action against Chechnya in the following year.[19]

In Dagestan, official Islam is represented by the Spiritual Directorate of the Muslims of Dagestan (DUMD). In September 2003, following the adoption of a new constitution, DUMD received official recognition as a public organization. The repulsed abortive invasion of 1999 had discredited its rival, Wahhabism, as DUMD and its Sufi/Sunni supporters call all fundamentalist organizations, including Salafists. Wahhabism was subsequently outlawed. Most Dagestanis because of this incursion and later attacks identified with Wahhabism (and Salafism) came to prefer Russian intervention as opposed to extremism. In fact, Wahhabism was outlawed on the day the invasion was crushed.[20] At the same time, all education at religious universities outside of Dagestan and Russia was placed under DUMD. This provision covered overseas education so that indirectly the government controlled higher education through its Islamic organ. Moreover, the registration must be approved by the republic's religious organization (|DUMD).[21] Failure to register through DUMD would result in penalties and fines. In essence, official Islam via DUMD became an organ of the government. In addition, in isolated rural areas, councils would be set up by DUMD.[22] DUMD staffed by Sufis became especially powerful in those areas where there was no federal or Dagestan official apparatus that functioned. In essence, because it has been placed in a political role, it has become politicized.[23] As corruption has increased as Moscow has governed through elites, access to aid has become increasingly inaccessible. At the top of these elites is DUMD which is simultaneously supported by Moscow but is also seen as an alternative to government.[24]

Subsequently, as the alternate to the deficiencies in the system, rather ironically the Sufi/Sunni have lost their traditional moderate orientation and become akin to the radical Islamists they accused their opponents — called

Wahhabis but often Salafists-of being.[25] Originally, in the late eighties through the mid-nineties, Wahhabism had appeared as an alternate to an existing situation. Until the Central Asian seminaries and overseas universities began turning educated and qualified graduates, they promised a superior clergy to replace ill-trained and ill-prepared clerics including imams, qadis, and ulama. Initially, to many, they appeared to offer a panacea to not only religious but also secular incompetence that prevailed in the "free-for-all" atmosphere that prevailed in the immediate post-Soviet period. They were supported liberally by the Saudis and other Gulf Arabs.[26]

They offered an ideal paradigm of a just society under strict Sharia rules governed by the Qur'an. They inveighed against the impurities that had crept into Muslim practice. They regarded the teachings of Sufis as "shirk" or polytheistic decay because of the acceptance of traditional customs and worship of saints and the ongoing corruption of the secular government as "un-Islamic."[27]

The new religious puritans also had support by people fed up with customs such as giving gifts to authorities in order to get things done. The various regulations from the Soviet period were cumbersome. The appeal of the Wahhabis/Salafis to get rid of them backed by Arab money as a cushion against oppression found support among the people.[28]

For a while, the Islamic Party of Revival which combined the objectives of Wahhabism with moderate outreach to the existing religious and secular establishment, was popular. However, its leader was attacked by both government and a more radical wing, and he died suddenly in 1998. His successors returned to radicalism.[29]

Ultimately, radical Islam became discredited for two reasons: its extremist views and the terror tactics it employed. First of all the puritanical approach it employed alienated young Dagestanis. Young people in Dagastan had grown up in a more tolerant atmosphere, and the strictures that were directed against alcohol and relations with the opposite sex did not favor with young people.[30]

It was, however, the violent acts of terrorism that led to disenchantment with Muslim extremists. There had been connections with the Chechnya as early as 1996 when the head of Islamic Wahhabis, Bagautdin Kebedov, organized Wahhabi cells in Chechnya. He later organized a brief secession called the Djamaat of Dagestan in central Dagestan. From this base, attacks were made in 1997 and 1998. His group and other groups were assisted by foreign fighters mostly Arab. Attacks continued through 2002 on a sporadic basis and still occasionally do today (as the recent attacks on Volgograd prior to the Olympics attest).[31]

The determinant event was the major invasion of Dagestan by Chechens aided by Dagestani radicals such as Kebedov whose organization of the Islamic Emirate of Dagestan (along with sister organization, the Islamic Emirate of the North Caucasus) still bedevils the region today. During this 6 and one half week invasion, 32,000 people lost their property and were made homeless and 13,000 people were killed or wounded.[32] This event discredited the Wahhabis and decided the Russians soon to be under Putin later in the year to assist Dagestan and intervene in Chechnya. Dagestani officials began to arrest anyone even suspected of terrorist activity. Today neither brand of Islam is popular in Dagestan (as DUMD is connected to corruption and the fundamentalists are connected to violence and terrorism). Whatever radical feeling that exists is tempered by the threat of Russian intervention (and to some extent Russian assistance which greases the wheels) as well as the example of the widespread carnage that took place next door in Chechnya.

Chapter 10

CHECHNYA

Located southwest of Dagestan, the Chechens are the most numerous of the North Caucasian peoples. They belong to the Vainakh peoples of which the Chechens and their close relatives the Ingush form the bulk of this group. Although converted relatively late to Islam (1500-1800),[1] they have, perhaps typical of the relatively newly-converted, been among its most zealous advocates. Similar to their Dagestani neighbors, they are Sunni and belong to the Shafi 'i law code as opposed to the more establishment Hanafi and Maliki law schools. Sufism has flourished in Chechnya as it has in Dagestan. As in other parts of the North Caucasus, the most prominent Sufi brotherhoods are the Quadiriyya and Naqshandiyya. The Sufi emphasis on individual communion with the Almighty appeals to the individualist nature of Chechens.[2]

In the resistance to Russian colonialism, the Murid movement of brotherhood followers was active in Chechnya as well as Dagestan under the same resistance leader, Shamil, between 1831 and 1859. Afterward, Chechnya was organized by clan structure and Islamic zealotry depended on the egalitarian characteristics of the society not class or aristocratic privilege hence the popularity of the tariqa or brotherhood. They did tend to use religion to differentiate themselves from the neighboring Christian Ossetians and Georgians.[3]

Chechnya, unlike Dagestan which had a reputation for Sufi learning after 1000 through its poets and philosophers, was not considered a center of Islamic learning. It had been a late addition to Islam and had a separate existence for nearly one millennium. It was already defined by its language and culture.[4] Nonetheless, Sunni Islam did have some impact on Chechen culture and society as it does provide prescriptive rules on law, government, economics, social customs, and most relevantly, military and political leadership. In 1919, Chechnya, along with Dagestan, opposed anti-Bolshevik forces as remnants of Tsarist rule. During this period, the town of Vedeno in Chechnya became the capital of a proposed North Caucasian Emirate. Vedeno had historically been a center of Islam for Chechnya (and indeed was a bastion of the Chechen radical Islamist rebel warlord, Shamil Basaev, who launched a military raid in support of an Islamic emirate in the Caucasus in August-September, 1999).[6] The Chechens were to remember the brief period of independence before the Bolsheviks/Communists took over in 1922.

After suppression during the Soviet Era including deportation (along with other nationalities to Central Asia and Siberia during WWII for 13 years before being allowed to return to ancestral homelands in 1957), Islam revived after 1990. However it was a revival based on traditional beliefs which had historically commingled with Islam. Traditionally, folk and ethnic customs had been preferred to the strict prescriptive formulae of Sharia and the Qur'an. As has been indicated, Sufism had arrived with Islam and had been more warmly welcomed. Sufism which recognized the role of custom in religious observance including the worship of saints and accepted syncretism had become the most common form of Islam.[7]

Although the Chechen conflict and its consequent outcome have served to solidify Islam especially the orthodox variety, it was only one of several identities of a Chechen at the end of the Soviet era. Typically, a Chechen might consider himself (or herself) a Sufi, a Sunni, a North Caucasian, a Vainakh, a clan member of which there were 150, a member of brotherhood (Quadiriyya or Nasqabandi), a highlander or lowlander, and a rural or urban dweller. Beyond this outer layer, a Chechen might characterize himself/herself as a member of a village or family or an educated person or not. By these criteria, a Chechen would differentiate himself from every other nationality Muslim or not except to some extent their neighbors the Ingush.[8] Even the identification with the Ingush was weakened when it was separated from Chechnya.[9] The intense identification with Islam as a or maybe the defining trait of identity is a recent development created by the crucible of strife.

In 1991, during the chaos of the break-up the Soviet Union and disillusionment with the local Communist apparatus the leaders of whom were in league with the coup plotters of August 1991 (along with a decrease in aid from Moscow), a rather suspect election was held and a former military officer, Dzhokhar Dudayev, was elected president.[10] Building on the tradition of Chechen independence and resistance to Russia, he declared independence in October 1991.[11] At this time, Russia was disorganized and military attacks that lasted from December 1994 until August 1996 were unsuccessful. However 100,000 people had perished and the capital Grozny had been basically leveled. So far, the conflict which continues today has cost over 200,000 lives. A temporary truce was signed.[12]

The first president had been killed in April 1996 and his successor, Aslan Maskhadov, who had been the military commander, was elected president in what was basically a one-party election with the military party in charge. During this period, two events happened: first, the country renamed Ichkeria was totally destroyed. The cities and villages badly damaged were not rebuilt. The country lacked basic sewerage, water, and electricity. Many schools were not functioning. The majority of the population had fled (those who could) so that the population had shrink from 1,270,000 in 1989 to 400,000 by 1996. Ironically, most ethnic Chechens were living in Russia. Chechnya became a center of criminal activity as it was the biggest producer, consumer, and distributor of narcotics and weapons in all of South Russia. Banditry, kidnapping, slave trading, and general lawlessness prevailed.[13]

The second (and ultimately decisive) development was the advent of Islamic extremism and terrorism. What had begun as a national instinct for independence in keeping with the national heritage had been taken over by Islamic fundamentalists. As early as 1993, Chechen freedom fighters were being trained in terrorist camps. This accelerated in 1994 as hostilities commenced with Russia. Arab Muslim guerrillas including individuals linked to al-Qaeda entered Chechnya (Chechens have also fought with Islamists overseas). Chechnya whose first constitution had defined it as an independent secular state underwent a transformation.[14] Supported by money from overseas, indigenous Islamic warlords Shamil Basaev and Salman Raduev gained more power while Saudi national Habib Abd al-Rahman later known as Emir al Khattab set up Wahhabi training camps in the country. Mercenaries from other nearby Muslim countries such as Azerbaijan arrived. As radical Islamist gained strength, the President with his authority challenged declared that Sharia law was the law of Chechnya and would be totally implemented. Although Chechnya had an employment rate approaching 70%, its oil and mineral wealth enabled Islamic rebels to raid neighboring republics (North Ossetia, Ingushetia, Dagestan, and Russia itself).[15]

By 1999, events were spiraling out of control. Newly-established Sharia courts began to pass sentences including flogging and mutilation and the individuals punished included children and pregnant women. Aid workers and two Russian envoys were kidnapped and murdered. [16] The period between

1997 and 1999 was the highpoint of extremism. Dagestan was the main objective. Chechen extremists joined by Dagestani extremists supported a secessionist Republic of Central Dagestan under Islam and attacked police stations and government offices. They called for the resignation of the Dagestan government and the departure of Dagestan from the Russian Federation so as to form the Islamic Emirate of the North Caucasus. The climax came with the invasion of Dagestan by extremists. The widespread loss of life and property between August 2 and September 16 provided a pretext for Russian action.[17] The acts of the Chechen extremists were now designated as a threat to the threat to the integrity of the Russian Federation (although in truth about 80% of the rebels were Dagastanis).[18] Any hesitation about action against Chechnya was eliminated by a series of apartment blasts in Russia itself and a bomb attack on military Russian housing in Dagestan in September Later that month, the new Prime Minister of Russia, Vladimir Putin, sent troops into Chechnya on the rationale of the need to attack terrorism, took Grozny in February, and imposed direct rule in May.[19]

In order to placate Chechen Muslims, Russia appointed a former Chechen cleric, Akhmat Kadyrov. as head of administration. After a new constitution was approved, which stated that the Chechen Republic was part of the Russian federation, he became President in 2003. After he was killed, two placeholders held the position until his son was old enough to take office as president in 2007. The son, Ramzan Kadryrov, supported by a militia accused by human rights groups of atrocities, remains in power supported by Putin.[20]

Nonetheless, violent clashes continue led by a new group of Islamists who have replaced the old generation of Islamists most of whom have been killed. These acts of terror and violence both inside and outside of Chechnya have continued to this day. The most frequent targets have been military targets and areas of mass transportation.[21]

The two most notorious incidents by extremists were the attack on a Moscow theater and the Beslan School incident. Chechen rebels seized a Moscow theater in October 2002. The theater held 800 people. When Russian troops stormed the theater after releasing gas most of the rebels were killed but also 120 hostages. Even more serious was the Beslan school hostage crisis from September 1 to September 4, 2004. In this incident, armed Islamic militants took over an elementary school in North Ossetia. Mostly Ingush and Chechen, they took over 1100 people hostage including 777 children. They demanded the independence of Chechnya and the departure of Russian troops from Chechnya. In the end, Russian security troops with tanks and rockets attacked the building. Although the hostages were rescued, at least 334 hostages including 186 children in addition to a large number of people injured and reported missing.[22]

Chechnya under its current Russian-backed warlord has recovered somewhat with substantial Russian aid. Although there is still a large Chechen diaspora, the population has now returned to about 1 million.[23] Even though there are still rebel attacks, much of the damage has been repaired and services have returned to normal.[24]

A major outcome of the over two decade conflict, however, has been the strengthening of Islam. Where formerly, the type of Islam observed was the Sufi influenced syncretistic form of Islam (and membership in Sufi brotherhoods was a means by which Chechens and Ingush retained their identity during their exile in Central Asia), the new emphasis is being placed on traditional orthodox Islam. The government has introduced practices which are perfectly consistent with Wahhabi positions. Women now wear hijabs even in urban centers. Girls and women who did not wear these garments have been attacked. Long sleeves and skirts worn below the knees are strongly encouraged if not mandated. Other Islamic strictures are enforced. Dating of unmarried women is strongly discouraged. Alcohol is in the process of being banned. There are prayer rooms in every school. Dozens of new mosques and Islamic institutes are now rising. Television has been instructed to devote a greater percentage of its programming to Islam. Gender segregation has been introduced in such commercial and public ventures as hair salons and gymnasiums.[25] Islam, despite the repression of separatist militantly Islamic groups, appears in a stronger position than it did in 1990.

PART VI: THE BALKANS

Much of the Balkan Peninsula was under Ottoman Turkish rule for nearly five centuries (from mid-15th to early 20th century). Such a long period of control has led to a Muslim presence in every country. The two areas where Islam has led a lasting imprint — the Albanian world centered on Albania, but also affecting other Albanian-speaking communities in Kosovo, Macedonia, the Preservo Valley in northeast of Kosovo, now in Serbia, the Albanian community in the Sanjak area between Serbia and Montenegro, the coastal area of Montenegro, and some sections of northwest Greece; and Bosnia-Herzegovina which will be considered in the next section.

Chapter 11

THE ALBANIAN WORLD

Albania proper, sometimes containing Kosovo, is inhabited by people descended from the ancient Illyrians, resisted the Ottomans the longest as it had a fabled resistance under Scanderbeg from 1443 to 1468. Yet both Albania and Kosovo accepted Islam more readily than other Balkan peoples (the Albanian peoples in other areas outside Albania proper world have a higher percentage of Roman Catholic and Orthodox congregants). It is somewhat paradoxical therefore that the Albanians should have such a high percentage of Islam compared to other Balkan peoples. One must look at the history of Albania. It was historically influenced by its neighbors and ethnic cousins, the Greeks from the east and the Romans from the west. It was ruled successively from the west as part of the Roman Empire and from the east by the Greek Byzantine Empire for a period altogether of almost two millennia. In consequence, the prevailing religious divisions at the time the Ottomans arrived reflect these two divisions. The clans to the north across the narrow Tyrrhenian Sea from the boot of Italy were mainly Roman Catholic while the clans adjacent to Greece were Greek Orthodox. To a much less extent, (as Muslims compose 70% of the population today),[1] these divisions remain. Geographical divisions remain within Islam. The north and central part of the country became orthodox Sunni as well as the urban areas while the Bektashi sect which is a combination of Sufi and Shia has gained traction in the south and in rural areas.[2] As a Sufi sect, the Bektashi appealed to the ordinary often uneducated Albanian as do other Sufi orders. It did not require knowledge of Arabic and consequently of the Holy Books such as the Qur'an and the Sharia law written in Arabic. There are other Sufi related brotherhoods such as Quadiriyya and Tijaniyya among others. Although the Sufi orders have been present for centuries, the Bektashi have been dominant. Although they all

102   Norman C. Rothman

gained support as Sufi orders elsewhere do by practicing a form of toleration toward other beliefs including Orthodox, Roman Catholic, and traditional beliefs and type of syncretism with traditional beliefs, the Bektaski gained the most favor as they were a somewhat Shia sect (actually pantheistic as they find G-d within nature and animals as well as within mankind.). But their advantage was their Shia status as it was a way to express opposition to the Sunni Ottomans without forsaking Islam. Not very different from the Ahmadiyya, they are considered heretical because they do not support the abstention from alcohol, veiling of women, or even praying in the direction of Mecca. These beliefs along with their tradition of tolerance fostered good relations with both Catholic and Orthodox.[3]

In spite of a strong sense of national identity and their initial resistance to the Turks, Albanians readily converted to Islam for a number of reasons. Many Albanians simply saw a better future as part of the bureaucracy and army of the vast Ottoman Empire. More than any other Balkan people, they rose to prominence in both areas. They furnished a number of Army commanders in the Turkish Janissary (armed military). They also furnished high government officials including grand viziers (or prime ministers). One Albanian clan, the Kaproulu, dominated Turkish administration in the 17th century with successive grand viziers. The founder of the Khedival state of Egypt was an Albanian who had risen to high command, Muhammad Ali.[4]

There were other reasons for the spread of Islam. In Albania as well as adjoining Kosovo and western Macedonia, there were economic reasons. Conversion to Islam meant relief from the jizya tax imposed on non-believers. The Bektashi were also influential here as their beliefs included a respect for Christian practices previously held by the people. Islam also appealed to Kosovar and Macedonian Muslims as it provide a link with fellow Albanians who had converted earlier thereby promoting solidary across borders. In addition, it differentiated Albanians from often antagonistic Slavs and Greeks and gave them an advantage in disputes which might be placed before the Ottoman suzerain. Eventually, it became a symbol of Albanian nationalism as it struggled against Pan-Slavic and Pan-Hellenic aspirations after 1800. These aspirations threatened both national identity and the territorial limits of Albania itself.[5]

In this century, perhaps in response to the above nationalisms, Albanians developed their own nationalism — pan-Illyrianism which sought to unite all Albanians under on flag. Islam was a key part of this agenda. After Albanian independence in 1912, the newly independent Albania which devolved into a monarchy tended to see Islam as a rival for authority but there was no active

The Albanian World

persecution. In 1925, the Bektashi in Albania became the headquarters of the movement when Ataturk outlawed the movement. In 1924, the Sunni religious establishment founded the Albanian Muslim Community (called the Albanian Islamic Community before 2004) in order to o represent the country's active mosques.[6]

After 1945, the coming of Communism to both Albania and Yugoslavia brought new challenges to the Islamic population. Albanians in both Kosovo and Macedonia were under pressure as they represented a rival ethnic group to the Serbs in Kosovo and the nearly Bulgarian Macedonian population. The pan-Slav movements in these areas actually solidified Muslim feeling in these areas. The Bektashi were less affronted by the attack by still Christian Slavs as they were very tolerant of Christianity (and in fact eat pork and celebrate Christmas and Easter — not unlike the Alevis of Turkey and Alawites of Syria)[7] and indeed a number of them or rather their ancestors had embraced Islam as a half-way house to avoid forcible conscription and the jizya tax. In addition, a larger percentage of the Albanian population remained Christian, Mother Teresa, an ethnic Albanian, for example, was born in Macedonia.[8]

Albania proper under Communist rule for forty-five years at first did not experience active persecution. However, in 1967, the Communist dictator, Enver Hoxha, declared Albania as the world's only atheist state, and active persecution commenced.[9] In the nineteen seventies alone, over 1200 mosques were destroyed or converted to other purposes.[10]

With the fall of Communism, the gates were opened. Islam revived not only in Albania proper but also in the other Albanian populated areas of the Balkans. The total population of the Albanian-inhabited districts outside Albania approaches the 3.2 million of Albania proper (not counting the millions in the Albanian diaspora in Europe and elsewhere) and the rate of increase of Albanian populations may eventually make it the largest ethnic group in the Balkans (with the possible exception of the Vlachs).[11]

It should be noted that the Albanian Islam perhaps because of the Ottoman background has been fairly low key and tolerant and never as a whole supported political movements such as a universal Caliphate composed of all members of the universal umma. In consequence, avowedly Muslim political parties have not been ubiquitous.[12] The uprisings that occurred in Preservo and Macedonia may have had Islamic support but the grievances were strictly local. In the former, the inhabitants had been part of Kosovo, but their district had been switched to Serbia after WWII.[13] The Albanians of west Macedonia had been subject to forced colonization by the Yugoslav state of Serbs and Montenegrins who had departed after the collapse of Yugoslavia, but

Albanians still felt a sense of discrimination from the Slav majority unsure of its identity (challenged by Greece and Bulgaria) and mindful of the possibility of an eventual Albanian majority due to higher birth rates.[14] As a consequence even with economic grievances added to cultural issues, the rare avowedly Islamic party has not earned great support. In Kosovo, for example, the Justice Party has allied itself with official Islam and its plank which called for the mandated teaching of Islam in schools did not get support. In the last election, for example, it only received 7.2% of the vote.[15]

In Kosovo, especially with money flowing in from Saudi Arabia and other oil-rich Arab states, there would appear to have been a fertile ground for Islamism. The Kosovo conflict of 1998-1999 had destroyed 40% of all mosques as well as other religious buildings. Arab money had flowed in to rebuild the structures, but it did not translate into votes. In reality, the only two movements in the Albanian world toward Islamism was the joining of Albania to the OIC (Organization of Islamic Cooperation) — the only European state to do so. In addition, in 2011, an Islamic university opened in the capital city of Albania, Tirana in 2011.[16]

Over the past two decades, Albanian Islam has undergone two stages. The first is the Arab stage; the second is the Turkish stage. After the collapse of the Communist regime, the Muslim Community Association revived but was low in funds. Young people who had no knowledge of Islam were now introduced to Muslim schools and mosques often run by Islamic and Arab strategies.[17] By the mid-nineteen nineties, young Albanian Muslims were sent to Arab and Muslim Asian countries for education.[18] in addition, Arab missionaries arrived to train new imams and distribute religious literature. They filled a gap caused by over four decades of atheism. By 2001, Arab money had built 400 mosques (out of 570 mosques in Albania) and ran all but one of the country's madrassas.[19]

The Arab phase began to wane between 1997 and 2001. In 1997, a socialist regime which included some figures identified with the old regime came to power after a financial crisis. Islamic organizations and foundations which backed Muslim madrassas and schools began to be monitored. This surveillance increased in 1998 when it was discovered when a cell of the radical Egyptian Islamic Jihad was discovered to be operating in Tirana. After September 11, 2001, there was a renewed scrutiny of foreign Islamic charities that operated in the country. If they appeared on US and UN lists as organizations suspected of having links or funding terrorists, they were closed down or expelled from the countries. Also, charities which did not have proper documentation or licensing also left or were expelled. Some left voluntarily.

These events left a residue of bitterness as financial support from these organizations had been a boon to the impoverished Albanian Muslims. In addition, a number of the younger Albanians who had been education abroad in a strict Wahhabist or Salafist environment or who had been influenced by missionaries from Saudi Arabia and Yemen felt that this was a Western-backed conspiracy to prevent the re-Islamization of Albania.[20]

Any claims of marginalization which some zealous Muslims advanced were countered by renewed Turkish support. Turkey through government and private organizations has stepped in to fill the vacuum. Turkey which is an Islamic state with a secular tradition is often advanced as a model for Albania. It has been so successful that Arab-educated imams now have only one of 30 members of the MCA administration as opposed to 29 out of 30 ten years ago.[21]

Turkish support is more palatable as Albania seeks membership in the EU as does Turkey and has been a member of NATO since 2009 as has Turkey. Moreover Turkey, unlike some Arab states, has not been identified with international terrorism. The long history of Albania under Ottoman control, the predecessor of modern-day Turkey, has resulted in a a similarity of views. The Ottoman Empire had a large Christian element in its population as does Albania and over a period of time made accommodation with them. In contrast, Arab countries that materially assisted Albania and other Albanian-inhabited areas such as Saudi Arabia and Yemen had virtually non-existent or invisible Christian minorities or in some cases such as Sudan which also supported foundations in Albania a tradition of hostility towards Christians. Turkey also had geopolitical reasons for supporting Albania. Albania and Greece have been at odds on a number of fronts. First, in 1943-44, Greece expelled many Albanian speakers (Chams) from their homes in Northwest Greece. Second, Greece does not recognize Macedonia which is over 25% Albanian. As Greece and Turkey continue to have problems especially over Cyprus, Albania can be used to outflank Greece. Bulgaria which also borders Turkey has also had issues with it. At one time, Turks made up over 15% of Bulgaria's population. In the last quarter of century, though, Bulgaria has expelled hundreds of thousands of Turks while Bulgarizing others. As Bulgaria claims that Macedonians are basically Bulgarians (which has some validity), Turkish support of both Albanians in Macedonia and Macedonia itself is a useful counter. It is popular domestically as Turkey is now the home of hundreds of thousands of displaced Chams and Bulgar Turks.[22]

The closer Turkish ties based on history and a less radical approach based on Albanian tradition have found more favor over the past decade. The

Turkish approach has involved both government and private entities. Dyanet which is the country's Muslim Affairs Department, has permanent representatives in the country who supervise assistance in cooperation with Albanian officials to assorted Albanian Muslim organizations. The government has its aid branch TIKA which among other projects gave money to the cash-strapped MCA to renovate its headquarters. The Dyanet also has assisted Albanians who want to make the Hajj-a task that had usually been offered by Arab charities and organizations in the past.[23]

Turkey has adopted a global approach in its private undertakings. Its private charities support both religious and non-religious schools so that it has garnered a wider appeal among the population. Particularly active has been the Gulen movement. Fethullah Gulen, the founder of the movement seeks to train people in modern sciences as well as the tenets of Islam. His goal is to re-interpret and renew Islam to meet the needs of a changing Islamic society. Reason and critical thinking are the most important ingredients toward reaching this goal. Students should be taught the past and prepare for the future. Skills needed for modernization and Islamic beliefs are not antithetical. His schools have spread to other Muslim countries especially the Turkic-speaking countries of Central Asia. As it has in Turkey and other Muslim countries in which it operates, it has enlisted support from many members of the business and professional elite. Its stress on modern education while incorporating secular values into Muslim worship along with Gulen's strong condemnation of terrorism has opened doors in Albania. Gulen has adopted a wide ranging approach in the schools it operates. It has built a series of non-religious schools from nursery to university which are run by a non-religious foundation. It also owns Albania's largest newspaper, the Zaman. At the same times, its religious foundation, SEMA, now run five out of seven of Albania's major madrassa religious high schools.[24]

The result of the two trends since 1990 in Albanian Islam is to open up new schools. Although Arabs have seen a relative decline in influence with the rise of the Turkish influence, they still have devoted followers and remain an important influence in major mosques. Many of the younger imams were trained in Arab universities and were also influenced by Wahhabis' ideas (Saudi Arabia, Yemen) and Salafist ideas (Egypt) as well as Sunni missionaries before 2001. They have followed the Hanbali and to a lesser extent, the Shafi'i school of thought while the traditional Albanian Sunni (and Turkey) followed the more mainstream Hanafi legal school.[25]

The Wahhabis have also spread their influence to other parts of the Balkan peninsula aided by mujahadeen fighters in the Bosnian war.[26] The Wahhabis

The Albanian World   107

have also established themselves in other aspects of the Albanian population in the Balkans such as the the Rasko and Polmje areas in southwestern Serbia (the Sanjak), and Razaje, Plav, and Gusinje in the northern Albanian districts of Montenegro. These radical Islamists have also set up shop in the capital of Kosovo, Prizren, as well as Tetovo, the center of Albanian settlement in Macedonia. Supported by Saudi Arabia, they are now contesting control with existing moderate establishment. In Novi Pazar, the capital of the Sanjak area, there was a shootout in November 2006 between moderate Moslems and these radicals as well as further incident since then.[26] In Macedonia, since 1992, Wahhabist and Salafist forces have entered the country and tried to seize control of the Sunni Muslim community. As there are huge financial interests at stake (since rich mines are located in the Albanian-populated sector of Macedonia hence the earlier attempts to plant Serb and Montenegrin colonists there), the prize is enormous in the struggle between moderate and radical factions.[27]

The struggle between moderates (characteristic of traditional Sunni Islam in Albania) and the radical elements which have entered with Arab training, Arab money, and Arab missionaries is often characterized as either a generational conflict or a conflict between pro-Arab and pro-Turk factions. It is accurate as a characterization, but there are other factors at work. There has been a new strain of radicalism as young Albanians who have been educated overseas in institutions which stress a more radical Islam such as Al-Azhar in Egypt and have a greater knowledge of Islamic holy books, have returned. Particularly influential in the Sunni community, imams trained overseas have gained influence in the mosques and have formed a radical mostly Salafist faction in the AMC. Older Muslims were often less educated, dealt with non-Muslims, were inclined to belong to local Sufi organizations which had brotherhoods such as Halvets, Tifais, and Sadis, and were syncretic in their relations with other groups including the hybrid Shia Bektashi.[28]

The Turkish faction would appear to be more in sync with traditional Albanian attitudes of Sunni toleration toward non-Sunni and non-believers. Nonetheless, there have been complaints about the requirement concerning the use of language. Intensive Turkish language courses have been imposed in madrassas take over by SEMA perhaps in some cases as an alternate to previous Salafi control. There is resentment that the foreign factions are buying influence within Albanian Islam. The Albanian Muslim community feels marginalized on occasion because of the superior resources of outside Islamic forces. The AMC is attempting to reemphasize Albanian roots in

Albanian Islam.[29] This reaction was also a response of the radicals to set up a rival religious organization — the Muslim Forum of Albania.[30]

The emphasis on the divisions ignores two factors. First, the Bektashi have rejected attempts to compromise their independence. They rejected attempts by Salafists to form a single pan-Albanian Islamic group which would incorporate the Bektashi. They have also rejected Iranian offers of money to support the Betashis as a fellow Shia group. As the Bektashi have a relatively tolerant pantheistic view of religion, they reject the militant radicalism of the mullahs.[31] On the Sunni side, the Saudi organization, the Taibah, has paid Bektashi in poverty stricken rural areas to convert to Sunni Islam.[32]

Nationalism has also appeared as a force in Albanian Islam. Many young Muslims, who have studied abroad in stricter Islamic universities in countries such as Qatar and Malaysia, have dedicated themselves to Islam. They do so with a caveat; they are dedicated to an Islam with strong Albanian roots. They feel dedicated to their nation through a dedication to Islam. Albanian Islam has always had strong national roots in spite of the influx of foreign influence (and resources) so that moderate versus radical has not overwhelmed Muslims in Albania. The Albanians throughout their history have adjusted their religion to the prevailing winds, but essentially the faith or version of the faith adopted has had an indigenous quality.

Chapter 12

BOSNIA

Bosnia or technically Bosnia-Herzegovina has been the other Balkan land in which Islam has flourished. By 1600, Muslims had become the largest single group in Bosnia. Even today, in spite of ethnic cleansing and genocide, they remain the largest single group. Unlike Albania which defines itself by language and culture, religion has become an integral part of Bosnia (Herzegovina is the southern one/fourth to one/fifth of the country which has occasionally enjoyed autonomy).[1]

Bosnia was susceptible to Islamic proselytizing for a number of reasons. Unlike Orthodox Serbia and Catholic Croatia, Bosnia did not develop a strong church organization. Second, the country was often torn apart by feuds between adherents of the two faiths which contributed to disenchantment by many Bosnians with both denominations. Accordingly, a third claimant for the allegiance of Bosnians appeared in a separate Bosnian church. These disputes led to a lack of overall fervor.[2]

Other factors made Bosnians susceptible to Islam during the 4 centuries of Ottoman rule. There was a kind of folk Christianity practiced. Native practices and ceremonies commingled with Christian services so that there was a large amount of syncretism. There was also the Bogomil sect. which began in Bulgaria but also spread to Bosnia. It some ways, it was similar to the Cathari movement in France in the 13th century in that it challenged some Christian doctrines and was similar to Islam. The Bogomils rejected the Cross. In accordance with that view, they did not recognize religious relics, saints, and any religious images. Perhaps most significantly, Bogomils prayed 5 times a day (as Muslim so) but used the Lord's Prayer.[3]

As was the case with Cathari and their offshoots, the Albigensians, there was persecution. Both the Bosnian Church and the Bogomils were accused of heresy. These accusations culminated in a Crusade launched by the Pope against the Bogomils in 1325 which also involved acts against the Bosnian Church as schismatic Earlier in 1231, the Hungarian state which at that time included Croatia, had cited the Bosnian Church as approaching heresy, and had launched a crusade as a pretext for annexing Bosnia. The Mongol attack on Hungary in 1240/41 preserved Bosnian independence for over two centuries.[4]

With this background, many Bosnians were attracted to Islam after the Ottoman conquest between 1463 and 1483. Most of the Bogomils became Muslims and the Bosnian Church adherents were divided among Catholics and Orthodox. As in the case of Albania, there were economic and social inducements. Converts to Islam could avoid the non-believer/jizya tax. In addition, under the feudal system established by the Ottomans, only Muslims could inherit land and property. As landowners, they would have certain social and political rights including the holding of local rights.[5] These landowners naturally would have no mandated military service except as commanders. Not surprisingly, landowners were among the first converts.[6]

Islam appealed to other segments of the population. As Muslims, it was easier to turn landholding into freehold tenure for peasants. Merchants were attracted as they had greater freedom of movement of goods and state protection for their goods. As cities were centers of learning, trade, and administration, urban classes were attracted. Many serfs (as well as peasants), joined the Ottoman military as well as the bureaucracy as a way of promotion in life.[7]

Overall, being a Muslim accorded an individual a higher status in society. You would have a higher standard of living as a Muslim especially if you were part of the Ottoman apparatus. Among the privileges that Muslims enjoyed over Christians were legal ones. For example, Christians could not sue Muslims, and their testimony could not be used against Muslims. There were no such restrictions against Muslims.[8]

Among the approximately 50% or so who remained Christian, there was a demographic shift which prefigured later divisions. The disappearance of the Bosnian Church meant that the Christian population was now divided between Catholic and Orthodox. The latter began to gain at the expense of the former. The Orthodox believers were favored by the Ottomans over the Catholics for a number of reasons.[9] First the Orthodox Church was under the secular government as was the case of Islam. There was no separation as in the west. Therefore, the Orthodox clergy easily accommodate their new Ottoman masters. The Catholics looked to an alien ruler, the Pope. Moreover, until

Russian began to stir in the 18th century, the foreign opponents of the Ottomans were Catholic — the Pope, the Holy Roman Empire, Poland -- as ruler of Ukraine at the time, and Spain in the western Mediterranean and coastal North Africa. The Ottomans reacted by allowing Orthodox churches to take over purely Catholic Churches. They were officially given control over all Bosnian Christians. In consequence, Catholics who did not emigrate to adjoining Catholic Slovenia and Croatia might be encouraged to join the Orthodox faith.[10]

Nevertheless, although there were religious differences and Muslims tended to receive a better education that prepared them for government service, there was relative amity. The Ottomans did not really wish wholesale conversion as it would reduce income by diminishing the number of people who could pay the jizya tax. Bosnia remained a predominantly rural society where both Christians and Muslims practiced syncretism wherein adherents of both faiths could intermingle their religious practices with indigenous customs. At this period, Bosnians still thought of themselves as a single entity rather than dividing themselves along religious/ethnic lines.[11]

It was the rise of nationalism in the 19th century that led to ethnic self-consciousness. Catholics began to be called Croatians (after the largest Catholic neighbor); Orthodox believers were called Serbs for the same reason (although not every Orthodox follower spoke Serb); the Muslims became Bosniaks. In actual fact, the language of Serbo-Croatian is the same orally. It is different in written scripts as the Croats (and recently the Bosniaks) use the Latin alphabet while the Serbs use the Cyrillic in writing.[12]

In 1878, Austria became the administrator of Bosnia and a modern educational curriculum was introduced. Muslims and Serbs were resentful as Austria was a Catholic power. After 1918, Bosnia became a part of Serb-dominated Yugoslavia. During the inter-war period, large numbers of Serbs were settled in Bosnia so that the Muslims ceased to be the largest group in Bosnia and their percentage shrank to 35%/ With WWII, this balance changed. After the Nazi takeover of Yugoslavia, the Nazi puppet regime of Croatia, the Ustashe, was given Bosnia and embarked upon a campaign of extermination against the Serbs. Orthodoxy was outlawed and both Catholicism and Islam were recognized as the only official religions. By some estimates, up to 500,000 Serbs were killed in Bosnia (and Croatia) as well as Jews, Gypsies, and anti-fascists. Up to 250,000 Serbs were deported and 200,000 were forced to convert.[13] A number of Muslims resentful of pre-war treatment did serve in the Ustashe military and government including as vice-president. In revenge, the Chetniks, Serb nationalists who favored a greater Serbia, killed almost

100,000 Muslims and even more Croats. As a number of Muslims died serving under Tito's multi-ethnic partisans and as most of the fighting of Tito's partisans took place in Bosnia against both the Chetniks and Nazis, the Bosniaks were spared reprisals. In fact, the half Croat half Slovene Tito when he established Socialist Yugoslavia in 1946 made Bosnia and Herzegovina one of six constituent republics in the reconstituted state. Now once again, inferior in numbers to the Muslims who they considered their greatest enemy within the federation next to the hated Croats, the embittered Serbs submitted as Tito believed that a weak Serbia meant a strong Yugoslavia.[14]

For a while it appeared that the ethnic/religious divisions had subsided. However, Bosnia was the only one of the six constituent republics without an ethnic majority. The three major groups within Bosnia had a dual allegiance (as Bosnian Yugoslavs, Serbian Yugoslavs, and Croat Yugoslavs respectively). In this manner, Bosnian Muslims identified themselves as both Yugoslavs and Muslims in the 1968 census.[15]

The break-up of Yugoslavia in 1990 had repercussions for the heterogeneous Bosnia. In 1990, Slovenia and Croatia seceded. Serbia, under the militant Slobodan Milosevic, embarked upon a greater Serbia campaign. Although the compact Slovenia beat back a Serb attack and the rather impoverished Macedonia was allowed to go its own way, Serbia embarked on a campaign to promote a Greater Syria which ultimately involved the end of autonomy for the Albanian-inhabited Kosovo and the mixed Voivodina, and outright aggression against Croatia and Bosnia when it declared independence in April 1992. After annexing parts of Croatia (regained by the Croats in 1995-6), Serbia used the Yugoslav army to assist local Serbs against the Bosnian Muslims now called Bosniaks.[16]

The multi-ethnic multi-confessional nature of the country has gradually changed due to the war which finally ended with the Dayton accords. It only came after much suffering mostly of the Muslims who were badly outgunned since western nations including the United States imposed an initial boycott on arms leaving the Serbs with all the resources of the Yugoslav military which they used. The Bosnian government started out proclaiming a multi-national state but was gradually forced by the exigencies of war and the pressure of the international community into adopting a sectarian approach of three communities although there had been some Croat and Serb support for a unified Bosnia. The war hardened these positions so that ultimately a divided federal solution was adopted. The Croats who had pursued a back and forth agenda; first siding with the Muslims then opposing them then back in alliance (there was a belief that there had been a pact to divide Bosnia into Croatian and Serbian sectors that Croatia went along with as compensation for Serb-speaking areas in Croatia annexed by Serbia; in other words, there would be a Greater Croatia along the lines of WWII along with a Greater Serbia). With the western blockage eased and Nato bombings of Serb forces in Bosnia after Serb atrocities had reached critical mass with bombing of civilians and the massacre of several thousand Muslim men and boys in Srebrenica and Goradje, Croatia took the offensive and reclaimed its territory.[17] With the expulsion of Serbs from enclaves in Slavonia (eastern Croatia) and Muslims from former Muslim areas (Banka Luka) in northern Bosnia and eastern Bosnia (Goradje), the partition of Bosnia into sectors based on ethnic religious affiliation was ratified at the Dayton Accords in 1996. The Bosnian-Croat Federation was given 51% of the territory which contained 63% of the population while the other sector, the Serb Republic had 49% of the territory and 37% of the population.[18] Although the reported population loss of 250,000 has been scaled back to less than half that, a large number of the country's people left so that it has about one/sixth less population.[19]

Most Bosnians still consider themselves as Europeans and religious moderates (and obviously they have other concerns as the present unrest in major cities over economic conditions indicates). As, however, Serbs made religion a part of their identification and Croats followed suit, Bosnian Muslims as Bosniaks have responded with religion as their own marker. The increased presence of religious fundamentalism is a byproduct of the war and the demarcation based partly on religion which accords with the goals of Islamists and political Islam.[20]

The war obviously had its effect. Nonetheless, the partial movement from the traditional rather cosmopolitan Ottoman version of Islam which emphasized at least a partial toleration of other religions within a common living space had been going on for several decades. During the nineteen seventies as party of Tito's non-aligned global focus, many young Bosnians were sent abroad to study at Islamic universities such as Al-Azhar. As a result, these young scholars returned with a more mainstream version of Muslim practices. They were much stricter in the observance of Islamic ritual and came to regard this observance including a more detailed knowledge of holy books as essential to Islamic identity.[21] The onslaught of Serb aggression which include ethnic cleansing, serial rape, concentration camps, bombardment of civilians and genocide (it occurred on the other side too, but to a lesser extent) based on hatred of their religion reinforced their zeal particularly as it seemed at one time during the Bosnian War with two/thirds of Bosnia occupied by Serbs and the other group, the Croats, unreliable and often hostile that they faced extinction (before NATO intervention). Subsequently, they regained some of their losses, and, with the Croats form a viable territory.[22]

The war had hardened feelings so that the ideal of a multi-denominational secular Bosnia faded. The intensified feelings grew in spite of long association among the three groups. Before the war, social mixing in spite of the memories of WWII had been common. Intermarriage had been frequent and had reached 40% in the urban areas before the war.[23]

Demographic facts had been created. As neighbor turned on neighbor, ethnic cleansing led to de facto apartheid. Muslim refugees took refuge in Muslim areas while Christian refugees (Croats and Serbs) did the same. Western media which often (out of ignorance about Bosnian traditions) portrayed the conflict at least initially as a conflict between civilizations added to an Islamic feeling of isolation. Many Bosnian Muslims came to feel that they were being driven from their homes and subjected to all sorts of indignities and atrocities because of their religion.[24]

The Islamic world responded vigorously to what was regarded as fellow Muslims being persecuted because of their religion, Money poured in from the Middle East, North Africa, and Southeast Asia. Volunteers came not only from Muslims in the former Yugoslavia such as Kosovo, the Sanjak, and Macedonia but also other parts of Muslim Europe such as Albania and Muslim parts of the former Soviet Union. The fundamentalist muhajadeen came from all over the Muslim world including the Arab world, Iran, and the Indian sub-continent (Afghanistan, Pakistan). Many young Bosnian Muslims were radicalized. In Afghanistan, for instance, after the Americans overthrew the Taliban, there were a large number of dead jihadis with Bosnian passports. During the Iraq war, there were Bosnian volunteers against the Americans.[25] There is some evidence that Al-Qaeda may be recruiting among Bosnian Muslims because their typical Caucasian features make them ideal as agents who could perform terrorist acts in Europe and North America.[26]

In spite of increased radicalism among Bosnian Muslims, the country does remain moderate at a steep economic cost. The Saudis, Turks, and others initially poured in a lot of money to support their fellow Muslims. The Saudi aid went to build mosques including the largest in the Balkans. Islamic aid went into the construction of the largest Islamic center and library in the Balkans. Often, though, the money was earmarked for the construction of religious buildings. The Saudis in particular spent much of their aid in the support and training of Wahhabist or those who advocated Wahhabi principles.[27]

Recently, because of the perceived moderation except for extremist pockets in the country, external Muslim aid has declined. This stems from the character of the Muslim-Croat Federation in Bosnia. The Federation practices separation of church and state and it does not have Sharia law (it is a federation with non-Muslims and the overall country has a bicameral legislature representing the three communities as well as a shared presidency). In addition, the educational system is secular. Because of these choices, Bosnia aid which is badly needed (it is poor with the highest unemployment rate in Europe)[28] no longer arrives to any degree from Muslim countries and western aid has not been sufficient.[29]

Bosnia Muslims were in some ways forced by external circumstances to identify religion with ethnic identity. Unlike their fellow Muslims in Albania and Kosovo, they do not have a separate language and culture with which to identify. As all three communities speak Serbo-Croatian, and historically have shared a common culture and undergone similar experiences, the current main determinant of ethnic identity for Bosnian Muslims (or Bosniaks as they have become known) is their religion.

PART VII:
THE MUSLIM DIASPORA IN EUROPE
(WITH CHAPTER 13)

The last two decades have seen an influx of Muslims in areas not normally associated with Islam. Russia which has indigenous Muslims in both the Volga/Ural region as well as the northern Caucasus has received an influx from former Muslim majority that were but no longer parts of the Soviet Union such as Central Asia and the southern Caucasus. When combined with the higher birthrate among Muslims, it is estimated that by 2030 Russia will have a population that is 14.4 % Muslim.[1]

Western Europe has seen a large migration of Muslims. By 2030, it has been calculated that France and Belgium will have over 10% of their citizens as Muslims. The statistics for other countries such as the United Kingdom, Germany, the Netherlands, and Austria are put at between 5% and 10% by 2030.[2]

Special historical circumstances may explain the upsurge of the Muslim population in Russia but other facts help to explain the increase of population in Western Europe. One reason is the colonial experience of some of these countries. In the United Kingdom, most Muslims have come from the Indian sub-continent which was under British control for much of the past two centuries (and between 1858 and 1947 officially). Among these South Asians, the largest number has been Pakistanis. In France, the largest number of Muslims has come from its former colonies in North Africa — and to a lesser extent, West Africa — with the largest number coming from Algeria and Morocco. In the Netherlands, most Muslims have come from the former Dutch East Indies (now Indonesia).

Other causes have included economics, humanitarianism, and geographical proximity. Economics has drawn many immigrants including Muslims to countries such as Belgium and Switzerland. Humanitarianism has often led to a resettlement of refugees to Austria and the Scandinavian countries of Denmark, Norway, and Sweden. Geographical proximity has led to the arrival of immigrants in Greece, Italy, Spain, and Portugal. Refugees such as Kurds, Palestinians, Bosnians, and Albanians/Kosovars as well a number of African Muslims from Nigeria and Somalia who are also drawn for economic reasons. Germany has drawn people for both economic reasons (through its guest worker program) such as the Turks as well as refugees from the former Soviet Union for humanitarian reasons.[3]

These new arrivals are not just young and mostly male who seek opportunity in Europe but also families. As was the case of the United States, there is often a chain migration and family reunification. One individual may be followed by later members of his family or groups. Urban areas are a special magnet. Moscow alone has 600,000 Muslims, and London, Paris, Stockholm, Brussels, and Amsterdam have similarly large Muslim populations. Most major cities now have specific sections for ethnic groups including immigrants.[4]

The basic issue in Western Europe (including both Northern and Southern Europe) as opposed to societies with a long history of Muslim habitation has been the process of accommodation if not assimilation between immigrants and the host society. This problem of adjustment is also present in eastern European societies with long familiarity with Muslims. The Bosnian civil war of 1992-96 as well as the Kosovo conflict of 1998-99 (previously covered in this work) was not only an issue of Bosniak vs Slav or Albanian vs Slav but also of Muslim vs. Orthodox. In Russia proper, Muslim-Orthodox relations have been aggravated by fundamentalism in the Caucasus. The arrival of militaristic politicized Islam during the past two decades has not only aggravated ongoing conflict (see the previous sections on the Caucasus) but also led to bloodshed and sectarian violence in Moscow itself where a number of terrorist acts have taken place. These have led to a xenophobic backlash on the part of Russians who would like Muslim arrivals not only deported from Moscow but also all of Russia. The issue of migration to Europe by immigrants including Muslims within the newly established European Union with 17 countries which allows passage from member country to another has intensified feelings. Therefore, a new arrival who enters Greece can wind up in Denmark. The coming of new arrivals with a second or even a third generations of young Muslims has put new pressure on societal adjustment as

Part VII: The Muslim Diaspora in Europe 119

host societies struggle with an increased challenge of integration in often stagnant economies. Countries known for toleration such as the Netherlands and Switzerland have considered restrictive measures. In fact, Switzerland just recently passed a referendum (very narrowly) which would restrict immigration. The issue will increase as Muslims have a higher fertility rate and a younger age structure than the general population.[5] The situation of Muslims in three major countries: France, Great Britain, and Germany will be discussed in the following sections.

Chapter 13

MUSLIMS IN FRANCE

Although Pew estimates the Muslim population at 10.3 % in 2030, other estimates go higher.[6] More significant is the degree of intensity. Perhaps typical of newly arrived groups, the percentage of Muslims who attend daily and weekly services is much higher than secular and nominally Catholic France. During the decade between 2001 and 2011 almost as many new mosques were built as churches although the population of Muslims at the time, was below 6 million.[7] By the latter year, 25% of the population of Marseilles(France's second city) was Muslim while the percentage of population of Strasbourg, the largest city in eastern France had reached 15%.[8]

Internally, the majority of French Muslims (about 80%), live in what are called "sensitive urban zones," often called "no-go" zones where law enforcement is somewhat problematic. When law enforcement attempts to exert effective control, riots break out. Today, over half of the prison population is Muslim. This situation and the overall lack of integration is the breeding ground for fundamentalism and terrorism.[9]

Overseas Muslim countries finance fundamentalist activities. Saudi Arabia, for example, finances the World Muslim League which is the international arm of the Muslim Brotherhood. Qatar also finances the Muslim Brotherhood's French arm, the Union of Islamic Organizations. Both the Brotherhood and the Arab sponsors support imams who preach radical theology from the mosques. The representative organizations such as the Union of French Islamic Organizations backed by the Muslim Brotherhood and the umbrella organization of the French Council of the Muslim Faith have tended to appeal more to the educated middle classes and students than to

122   Norman C. Rothman

those segments of the Muslim population such as the workers and lower classes who have the most grievances.[10]

Recently, when the then current president, Nicolas Sarkozy, proposed new requirements for citizenship based on language, culture, and adherence to French "values," the Muslim population turned against him. They supported his victorious opponent, Francoise Hollande. After his election in 2012, Hollande supported the transition of a number of "no-go" zones into priority security zones so as to reestablish authority.[11]

In France, there have been a number of incidents which highlight the tense situation of Muslims in France. In the fall of 2005, young Muslims rioted for 18 days. Although the attention of the word was focused on Paris where much of the rioting took place, violent demonstrations also took place in Lyons, Toulouse, Lille, Nice, and other cities. During this spasm of rioting, 8700 automobiles were burned, and 360 were trashed.[12] In addition, 140 buses, 255 schools, 233 public buildings, 100 post offices, and at least 20 private residences. All told, hundreds of millions of dollars of property were damaged, and over 5,000 people were arrested.[13]

The causes of these outbreaks were primarily economic. They were a protest against the preferential treatment unionized workers –native French and white — while immigrants got short shrift. Unlike the unionized workers who usually have lifetime security and 35 hour weeks, annual 6-week vacations, and an early and generous retirement package, many immigrant workers, chronically unemployed, do not receive these benefits which also include a health plan which the World Health Organization has rated the best on the world. Many of the rioters were second generation Muslims who lived in slum-like conditions and go to underfunded overcrowded schools unlike their French non-Muslim counterparts.[14]

The areas in which these immigrants live called "banlieu" are slums in which many people are unemployed. They are really "no-go" zones with substandard housing and with minimal law enforcement. They are suburbs which ring urban areas and are isolated from them. There is minimal transportation wherein it may take one hour to go from the suburb/banlieu to the city where jobs may be and the same time coming back. Often the layout of these sectors is composed of bleak concrete structures. These sectors are short in amenities. They may lack movie theaters or shopping malls and other modern conveniences that make life bearable for young people. These suburbs are often separated from cities by speed bumps that increase their isolation.[15]

In these isolated ghettos, young people may feel that they face a dead end existence. Quite often, these second or third generation people feel caught between two worlds. They are not at home on their somewhat rare visits to North or West Africa. Yet, at the same time, they face or feel they face discrimination in France as opposed to "French." With this background, many young Muslims are susceptible to Wahhabis or Salafis who promise a panacea.

Moreover, the headscarf or hijab controversy has roiled France for over a decade. As early as 2002, there were reports of young Muslim women with uncovered or unveiled faces being harassed by other Muslims. The use of veils and hijabs was often considered a defense mechanism for preservation of chastity.[16] It can also be interpreted as an act of faith or submission to Allah, In the early twentieth century, the custom had somewhat receded as many countries including Islamic ones underwent modernization. In recent decades as slamization has increased, it has revived as an issue.[17]

In 1989, the issue of wearing the headscarf in officially secularist France became a controversy when the principal of a high school expelled a student for wearing a headscarf. The matter reached the State Council, the supreme administrative court, which decided that the hijab could be worn as a gesture not as propaganda. Eventually, the executive branch decreed that it was up to the principal or dean if it was a college or university to decide if the hijab was worn for faith or propaganda and act accordingly. This was not the end of the matter as in 2004 it was concluded that headscarves violated France's secularist policies.[18]

Ultimately in 2007, the law was revised so that the ban against headscarves would only be required in publically funded primary and high schools. It does not cover universities or religious schools. Students at universities can wear these hijabs as part of freedom of expression and religion as long as it does not violate public order. It should be noted that the law also bans Christian crosses and Jewish yarmulkes (skull caps) in terms of secularism.[19]

Another issue which relates to Islam in France has been the ongoing attacks on symbols of Judaism. Official reports have indicated an increase in anti-Semitism. In 2000, for example, anti-Semitic attacks went from 12 a month in September- the previous month — to 418 during October. It was made clear by most of the perpetrators that it was connected to the Intifada uprising among Palestinians which reignited that year during the fall. Partially, as a consequence, immigration of French Jews to Israel jumped to 12,000 during the next few years. These attacks (80% were traced to Muslim extremists although France has a history of anti-Semitism) often appeared (although not always) to wax and wane with events in the Middle East. In this respect, there was a noticeable spike in anti-Semitic incidents in France after the Israeli incursion into Gaza in December 2009 and January 2010.[20]

Anti-Semitic incidents took various forms which could include threats or attacks in men wearing yarmulkes, burning of synagogues, desecration of Jewish cemeteries, and graffiti including swastikas placed on walls of Jewish homes and businesses. Sometimes, there were instances of extreme violence. The most notorious of these violent incidences occurred in a schoolyard in Toulouse in March 2012 when a rabbi and three young children were killed by a Muslim extremist. A study conducted in 2005 found that 46% of practicing Muslims in France had anti-Jewish prejudices.[21]

The French whether at home or in their overseas empire have adhered to a policy of assimilation. Ethnicity has no place in France whether it is a group or overseas territory or religion. This attitude has affected second or third generation Muslims who feel locked out of the French society and economy.

Chapter 14

THE UNITED KINGDOM

In recent years, the largest component of immigration in the United Kingdom has been through immigration. It is estimated that between 1990 and 2030 there will be a five-fold increase in the Muslim population so that there will be 5.5 million out of 68 million that profess Islam. The increase will be due primarily to immigration especially from the countries that emerged from British India such as Bangladesh and Pakistan.[1]

Various other demographic factors point to a greater Muslim role in Great Britain and the potential challenges that it entails. Because of higher fertility one out of every 10 Britons under 25 is Muslim. Various surveys indicate that Britain is the least integrated of the major societies. In 2010, only 15% of the country's Muslim population considered themselves British as opposed to 75% who considered themselves primarily Muslim. The contrast was even starker in a 2006 Pew Survey in which only 7% considered themselves as British first while 81% considered themselves Muslims. The equivalent figures for Germany were 13 and 68 while that of France was a nearly even 42 and 48% respectively.[2] It appears that in spite of assimilation policies in France and, to a lesser extent, Germany with little tradition of immigration, there was less overall alienation The British model of allowing communal leaders to represent their communities as opposed to a more centralized approach in France, and, to a lesser degree, Germany has resulted in a somewhat paradoxical result — a greater vulnerability to jihadi and terrorist influences. It appears that the British tradition which has allowed local cultural nationalism to flourish in Scotland, Ireland, and Wales as opposed to Brittany, Corsica, and Normandy in France, and the Rhineland, Bavaria, and Saxony in Germany which, allowing for local pride, has not reached the point of departure as in

Ireland in the past century, Scotland perhaps this year, and Wales which has revived its language, has produced this result. It appears that overt emphasis on multi-cultural policies has caused less integration. Other countries may see Muslim frustration over perceived lack of opportunity, but many Muslims in Britain feel rage over multi-cultural rhetoric and social reality. The last census indicated that 1,000,000 had converted to Islam. Taken together with these factors, it is not inconceivable that the number of people who profess Islam may approach those who profess Christianity. This circumstance arises from surveys that show that less than one/half of young people identify themselves as Christians. Christianity, evidently, has become the religion of people over 60.[3]

Many young Muslims in Great Britain have been radicalized (which has had more violent incidents than in France or Germany). There have been two sources of this radicalism. The first comes from radical groups financed as elsewhere by Saudi Arabia and other Gulf states for Sunni and Iran for Shia. It is compounded of anti-imperialist attitude (usually directed at the West particularly Britain), religious revivalism (back to the original purity of Islam), and a jihad against what is perceived as creeping secularism.[4] The fundamentalist drive has taken two forms. The first is the Wahhabi movement which combats what it terms pollution by practices such as the visiting of shrines and the worships of saints and the visits to tombs often identified with Sufi rites.[5] It emanates from and is financed by Saudi Arabia. Related to Wahhabism is the Salafi movement which has been supported primarily from Egypt. Salafism is less concerned with combating pollution than with returning to the "golden age" of the original Islam and the activities of Muhammad and his followers or Salafi.[6]

More germane to the British experience are Islamic groups that derive from the Indian sub-continent –the home of the largest Muslim population in the world (approximately 500 million). These organizations include the Deobandi movement, the Tabligh Jama'at known as the TJ, the Group for the Preaching and Propagation of Islam, the Jama'at-i-Islami or JI, the Islamic Bloc, and the Muslim Brotherhood. The Deobandi is a fundamentalist group which operates seminaries and brotherhood and is active in India and Pakistan.[7] The Muslim Brotherhood — a world-wide group was founded in 1928. It attempts to translate Salafi ideals into political action. It is considered the establishment fundamentalist group.[8]

All three countries (Britain as well as France and Germany) experienced a labor shortage because of World War II. During this period of boom they were actively recruited by employers.[9] The availability of work was attractive especially when times were hard at home. Chain migration would occur as although wages were relative low for migrants in Britain, they were thirty times the average wage in Pakistan. To encourage this migration, temporary visas and work permits were issued. This system was in place in Britain between 1948 and 1962.[10] Ultimately, this proved a road to citizenship for many people from across the globe who received "commonwealth preference." The practice was meant to encourage white people from Australia, Canada, and New Zealand, but it was used most frequently by natives from the West Indies, the Indian sub-continent, and to some extent, Africa.[11] By the time, this policy was rescinded in 1962, secondary migration had occurred as relatives of earlier immigrants arrive based on family reunification.[12]

Integration never took place as Britain, unlike America, was not a melting pot for immigrants including Muslims. Overseas through indirect rule and at home through home rule for Scots, Welsh, and Irish, cultural identity was stressed over assimilation. Just as the British had administered their empire through traditional authorities, emigrants arriving in Britain were encouraged to look to their community leaders. These leaders which included for Muslims the imams in mosques became the local intermediaries between communities and the government.[13]

Ultimately, this policy promoted divisions. The emphasis on promotion of "values" as oppose to cultural integration proved negative. Groups kept their cultural identity, but the social system remained closed. With economics in decline especially after 1975, the ingredients for discord in Britain were there. Muslim dignitaries were assigned the task to meet community needs. Under this policy, Britain allowed the use of Sharia courts in parts of the country with heavy concentrations of Muslims. Radical preachers were allowed to preach jihad from mosques without much interference from authorities. Certain sections of major urban centers such as Leeds and Manchester had sections which were autonomous (and still are).[14] London with a Muslim population approaching 600,000 became known as Londonistan. As time went by, this acceptance along with limited life opportunities led to violent outbreaks acts more virulent than on the continent. The climate of acceptance not only allowed virulent incendiary rhetoric from the mosques but at bookstores, in newspapers, in journals, and other outlets of public media.[15] Extremist groups that had been outlawed in other countries in Europe and the Middle East now set up shop in Britain. These included the Libyan Islamic Fighting Group, the Islamic Jihad, the Gamaa Islamiyya, and the Islamic Fighting Group. So many terrorist groups had migrated to London that it had earned the sobriquet of Londonistan bestowed originally by French security officials after the mastermind of The Algerian Islamic Group (GIA) planned terror attacks from London.[16]

By the mid-nineties, under the official contract of allowing Muslims to be represented by communal leaders to preserve order which entailed Muslim domination of local councils where there were majority Muslim populations and Muslim representatives in Parliament, a dual situation had arisen whereby these sanctioned leaders represented the Muslims without any reference to Britain, Some of these leaders were extremists who functioned under what was called " blanket of security" including 4 preachers who became known fir preaching among other things such as subversion, anti-Semitism, and homophobia. These preachers were to serve as enablers of terrorism in the next decade. They became known collectively as the "lords of Londonistan." They were to set the atmosphere for the extremists both in Britain and overseas. Ultimately they were deported or jailed when the British authorities cracked down during the following decade, but the fuse had been lit. The four were Abu Qatada, the direct inspiration of the 9/11 pilot and identified by the United Nations Security as a spiritual envoy of al-Qaeda who became the leading Jihadist in England and a special apologist for Algerian terrorist acts; Abu Hamza who presided for over a decade at the Finsbury Park mosque which soon gained the reputation of being London's most radical mosque; Abdullah el Faisal, a Jamaican convert who became the mentor to such notorious figures such as Richard Reid, the shoe bomber, Zacarias Moussaoui, the twentieth hijacker on 9/11 who was apprehended before the event; and Umar Farouk Abdulmutallab, the notorious would-be underwear bomber; and Omar Bakri whose party set up an underground railroad to Pakistan to train second and third generation British Muslim suicide bombers and was instrument in setting up an affiliate of what became the leading extremist organization, the Hizb ut Tahir (or HT). Other radicals who congregated in London at this time include Anwar Al-Awlaki who was there from 2002 to 2004 before he left for Yemen and began his infamous video recordings which still are in use after his death in September 2011.[17]

The negative effect of multiculturalism combined with neglect of younger Muslims in education and employment and the tradition of hospitality toward refugees in which refuge was given to extremists in return that they would not attack from Britain's shores and would self-regulation for this "blanket of security" which was repeatedly violated became apparent.. It was obvious when both immigrant and British born Muslims united against Salmon Rushdie's *The* Satanic *Verses.* The hostility took various forms such as demonstrations, book burnings, threats of violence against bookstores which

The United Kingdom 129

sold the book, threats against its publisher, and threats to carry out the "fatwa" that had been issued against Rushdie's life. Some members even of the Labor Party anxious for Muslim votes reacted to the actions not by condemning it but by promising single-sex education and state financed Muslim schools.[18]

Native born Muslims had the highest rate of unemployment, the lowest percentage of men in white collar jobs and as a corollary, the highest rate in manual labor, the highest rate of dropouts, and the most likely to live in poor housing. In every measure, Hindus and Sikhs did much better. The differential result among South Asians has been attributed to their insular existence arising from continued links with their home villages often in rural traditional areas which are more bound by custom as compared to the Hindus and Sikhs.[19]

The sense of less than fair treatment has been aggravated by external events. The massacre of 8000 men and boys at Srebrenica in 1993 was a traumatic event for many young British Muslims.[20] They also felt aggrieved by the invasions of Iraq and Afghanistan which they interpreted as attacks on Islam. A number of young British Muslims had studied overseas and came back with radical leanings. A number had even gone to terrorist training camps in Afghanistan and Pakistan.[21]

Those Muslims who did go on to education would come into contact with Wahhabis and Salafists. In addition, there were homegrown associations such as al-Muhajiroun which had split off from HT.[22] With more educated English speakers there was "fitna" or discord between young and old as the latter demanded native English speakers rather than imams from Pakistan or Iran (for Shia).[23]

The presence of so many terrorist groups such as the GIA, GI, the LIFG, and the TJ on British soil led to increasing radicalization. In 2007, it was estimated that were 4,000 individuals engaged in terrorist or related activity.[24] The following year, in a MI5 report it was reported that most religious radicals were between 18 and 30. Furthermore, there were some 200 terrorist networks which operating in the United Kingdom. Although London, Birmingham, and Manchester were designated as radical centers, the threat was located throughout the country.[25]

A series of violent episodes have indicated the extent of radicalism among Muslim youth. In August 2006, a plot was uncovered which involved 24 terrorists mostly young Muslims in a conspiracy to explode 10 transatlantic airliners traveling between Britain and the United States. If this plot had succeeded, there would have been fatalities greater than 9/11. Last year, an unarmed British soldier was stabbed and beheaded when he was attacked by two West African extremists.[26]

In Britain as in France, there has been a series of Muslim sections that are apart from other sections. In part, multicultural policies have encouraged segregation. There is even a group called Muslims against Crusaders which calls for the setting up of autonomous microstates within Britain under Sharia law. Another organization, the Islamic Emirates wants separate states within Britain (and elsewhere) outside of national jurisprudence. In fact, in Britain (as well as in France), there are a number of enclaves within municipalities where the host nation has lost control and basic services such as police, fire, and ambulance services are arranged through local community leaders. In some case, Sharia is used to mediate disputes among Muslims. East London is an example of these enclaves. Threats are made against women who refuse to wear veils. Any street advertisement that is deemed to be offensive to Muslims is defaced. (France is still the leader of such zones with 751 Sensitive Urban Zones).[27] These zones are also appearing in other European countries (see the following section on Germany). Through a combination of self-segregation and misapplied multiculturalism, many young Muslims feel marginalized in Britain, The consequences of this feeling is potentially dangerous.

Chapter 15

GERMANY

In comparison with France and Great Britain, Germany has had a more continuous robust economy based primarily on exports. Consequently, the economic causes of discontent are relatively less. Nonetheless, they are other issues in addition to economics which affect Muslims in Germany.

Originally, though, economic reasons were the cause of immigrations from Muslim countries mostly from Turkey. Due to the vaunted "German miracle," actually West Germany before reunification in 1990, more workers were needed. Germany had experienced huge losses in manpower during WWII and required additional labor if the economy was to function. The Iron Curtain separated it from a possible source of labor, and the problem intensified after August 1961 when the Berlin Wall was constructed thereby cutting off (West) Germany from another source of labor (mostly East Germany). Workers from southern Europe proved insufficient to fill the gap, Therefore, labor from Muslim countries, mostly if not exclusively Turkey, became common, By 1974, they constituted the majority of immigrant labor, Under the guest worker program, agreements were made with employers with government support.[1]

The understanding behind the agreements at the outset was that guest workers would stay for two years and then rotate back to their homeland usually Turkey after two years. Residency was tied to employment. This understanding turned out to be baseless as the pattern families joining the original migrants evident elsewhere was replicated in Germany. The result was not only the explosion of Muslim numbers but of Islamic symbols such as mosques which soared to 2200 by the mid-ninetees.[2]

The world-wide recession of 1973 did eventually affect Germany and its need for labor. By then; however, legal protections for guest workers included residence. Guest workers were given permanent residency rights even if employment ended. In 1978, it was further decreed that workers who had stayed a long time. They had "protected" status.[3] The desire to legally protect migrant workers perhaps somewhat rooted in the Nazi past was apparent. After the Munich Olympic massacres when 11 Israeli athletes and a German police officer were murdered, two Palestinian students with ties to the terrorists were deported, The case was appealed, and the Constitutional Court ruled that foreigners resident in Germany had private rights which outweighed state interests and therefore could not be deported.[4]

As the years have gone by, the question of integration has arisen. Second and third generation Turks (the predominant Muslim group) have not been integrated. This situation is due to both German views on citizenship as well as Turkish endogamy. Unlike France and Great Britain, Germany has not defined itself so much by culture and religion as by ethnicity through blood and ancestry. This approach persisted even after WWII when ethnic Germans returned from the East including the former Soviet Union, Poland, Czechoslovakia, the Baltic States, Hungary, and Romania, Even though most of these millions had been a part of groups that had spent centuries outside of Germany and many did not even speak German, they were eligible for citizenship

In contrast, second and third generation Muslims (two/thirds were Turks) numbering about 4 million by 2010 did not always qualify for citizenship. It was not until 2000 that Germany liberalized its naturalization/citizenship law. Citizenship was now to be based on territory not blood. Even then, a distinction was made between ethnic and non-ethnic Germans. Non-ethnic Germans still had to wait fifteen years in a probationary residence status as opposed to instant citizenship for ethnic Germans. The catch was that it only applied to people born after December 31, 1999 so that many young Muslims were left out in the cold. They had no immediate prospect of citizenship and, as will be shown, limited economic and educational prospects. Ultimately they became embittered as they, having been born and raised in Germany, were reminded of their indefinite status when infrequent visits felt like visiting a foreign land. At the same time, their lack of citizenship in the land of their birth left them susceptible to the siren call of radicalism.[5]

The relative sequestration of Turks has had its effects on societal integration. In part, this is due to the place of origin. The original migrants from Turkey came from urban areas and western Turkey, and so had some familiarity with European society as well as some modern skills. Beginning in the 1970's, the bulk of immigrants were from rural eastern Anatolia which has a stronger folk and Muslim tradition, They had fewer skills, and when chain migration began, it was possible for whole villages and kinship networks to migrate in its entirety to new homes in Germany. Arriving there, they tended just to associate with people of their own place of origin rather than society at large. In Germany, the same cultural and social patterns were reproduced. Marriage patterns reinforced this lack of integration. The bulk of marriages are within the Turkish community (one study estimates that over 90% of Turks marry other Turks). There is also a tendency to marry cousins. Consequently, Turkish is spoken in the home so that only 40% of second generation Turks is fluent in German as opposed to 80% second generation immigrants from the former Yugoslavia,[6]

The repercussions of the relative isolation which propel many Muslims (Turks and non-Turks) to permanent underclass status are apparent in education and economy. It is has been found that as many as 80% of Turkish first-graders have no knowledge of German with disastrous results for future learning. Because of deficient language skills they are often placed in special schools. Moreover, the dropout rate is nearly three times as great for Turks as for ethnic Germans. This differential follows students throughout the educational career. Twenty-five percent of native Germans attend the college preparatory track as opposed to six percent of Turks.[7]

The educational deficiency translates into economic deprivation. Germany has an efficient vocational track so that low skill jobs such as house painting, mechanics, and hairdressing are available especially within the Turkish social networks. At the other end of the spectrum, they are less likely to be in higher skill occupations, 40% of Turks have no vocational qualifications — five times higher than native Germans, and an unemployment rate of 18%.[8]

The degree of integration can be measured by a number of indices. Criminal suspects of Turkish origin are five times the number of those of Italian, Polish, Romanian, and Serbian origin.[9] A number of surveys indicate that Turks lag behind all other immigrant groups as well as native Germans in education, earnings, and employment. This is due to lack of knowledge of German which traps people into an inferior school track and job. Many people of Turkish extraction often do not feel the need to acquire German Approximately three/quarters live in Turkish sections surrounded by mosques, Turkish shops and restaurants, and professional services such as dry cleaning, and beauty shops which cater to a Turkish-speaking clientele. Turkish TV is available as are, on occasion, movies.[10] In short; many do not feel a compelling need to learn German as they can exist in their own secluded world without it.

The end result is a feeling of marginalization and alienation. Turks subsequently have turned to religion as a way to fill out a rather uncertain identity. A recent survey indicates that young people from 18 to 30 went from 63% to 80% in describing themselves as devout Muslims.[11]

The German alliance with the United States in the invasion of Afghanistan against (where she provided 2000 troops) against the Taliban and Al-Qaeda combined with the discontent of Young Muslims and their increasing religiosity provided a fertile field for radical Islam. They took advantage of German opposition to the war and in fact al-Qaeda and other terrorist organizations openly ran videos against German involvement in Afghanistan in the 2009 election. In general, the last decade has been marked by the appearance of Islamic groups including radical groups: the three operating in Turkey as opposed to less extremist fundamentalist and Sufi/Sunni groups: The International Islamic Missionary Movement (TJ)is not directly linked, but it puts many young people on the road to radicalism. Al-Qaeda was active in Germany but garnered few recruits perhaps because it was basically an Arab organization so it worked directly with Islamic Jihad Union (IJU). This organization is an offshoot of the IMU (the Islamic Movement of Uzbekistan), the foremost Islamic radical association in Central Asia. This Uzbek organization split off from the IMU as it wanted to pursue jihad across the globe against the infidel. It cooperates in this respect with the Taliban in Afghanistan and with Al-Qaeda training camps in North Waziristan.[12]

By 2005, Germany had its equivalent of Londonistan in the twin cities of Ulm, Baden-Wurttemberg and Neu Ulm, Bavaria which housed Turkish enclaves as it does in cities like Berlin, Frankfurt, Mainz, Mannheim, and Stuttgart. There, front organizations such as the Islamic Information Center in Ulm and the Multikultur Haus, recruited radicals in conjunction with the IJU which as a Uzbek organization is intelligible to most Turks as Uzbek is a Turkic language. They were eventually closed. [13]

In spite of the feeling of Turkic Muslims, many Germans remained oblivious to possible outbreaks. They claimed that the Turkish community was quiet and hardworking. They dismissed outbreaks such as the planning of 9/11 by an Al-Qaeda cell in Hamburg and attempted terrorist incidents in 2004-2006 as Arab-inspired and not related to the homegrown community, Yet, if they felt complacent about the possible outbreak of terrorism in Germany, they did not feel warm to immigrants in spite of the complacency. In a survey conducted by Pew in 2005-6, interviews were conducted in the three countries with the most immigrants: France, Great Britain, and Germany. In these countries, the negative view of immigrants were 41, 32, and 59 percent respectively.[14]

The complacency of Germans was basically shattered by the Sauerland plot of 2007. The Sauerland cell of the IJU plotted to kill 150 American soldiers in Germany. The plot failed, but another aspect of the plot shocked many Germans. All but two of the 40 plotters were ethnic Turks (the other two were German converts to Islam).[15]

The last incident has opened debate as to what constitutes identity and citizenship in Germany. Conservatives argue that both national identity and citizenship should rely on knowledge and understanding of language, law, and history. The liberals argue that national identity and citizenship should be based on democracy and human rights, Except for language, the left said the republic of Germany should be open to anyone who is willing to accept the rules of a particular nation such as Germany. Anything else would be discriminatory. When some citizenship tests were introduced in some states which required knowledge of certain cultural issues, they cried foul.[16]

The decision in regard to this argument has obvious implications for what is now Germany's largest minority as ultimately it will deal with Muslim access to citizenship and sense of identity.

PART VIII: CONCLUSION

The role of Islam in African and European societies depends to some extent on local traditions and contemporary circumstances. In many of these societies, the Sufi tradition and the existence of brotherhoods is evident. Since most of the societies covered — except for southern Azerbaijan — are Sunni societies, the role of Islamic clerics are important but not always overwhelming. The notable exception to this development was in the Fulani Jihads of the 18th and 19th centuries in West Africa, and, to some extent, in connection with the brotherhoods 19th resistance to colonialism in the Caucasus and North Africa. In all cases, the exclusivist aspect of the role of clerics in the society did not last beyond two generations.

Islam in contemporary Africa and Europe in unfamiliar non-establishment forms such as the fundamentalist Wahhabhi/Salafist manifestations and radical often violent groups such as the HT, the Muslim Brotherhood, the MUJAO, the Shabaab, Boko Haram, and Al-Qaeda in its various manifestations and affiliates have fed on discontent. This discontent has a number of causes. The latter can be classified as social, economic, political, and psychological /perceptual (the feeling and belief of unfair treatment and discrimination). It has both indigenous roots in the local culture but also artificial external backing usually financial and organizational. In the end, though, the type of Islam that emerges is determined by local conditions.

There are some generalizations that can be made although as with most generalizations there are exceptions. First, Islam has shown longevity even if not indigenous to Africa and Europe. It has survived even in the case of modernization which appears to run counters to Islamic principle. Its survival because its basic precepts cover a variety of topics — social, cultural, economic, political, legal, even military — from which people pick and choose.

Second, Islam reflects the religious, social, and cultural contexts in which it exists. Although periodically, there are attempts to "purify" Islam, Islam has continued because it in many cases appeals to hybrid conditions; it is open to syncretism. Many practitioners find that they can combine with local pre-Islamic and non-Islamic customs — folk Islam.

Third, although Islam is often considered "hard" and not absorbing as, for example, Buddhism and Hinduism, it is multiple in its incarnations. Under this rubric, there is the standard Orthodox approach of the Sunni, the somewhat heterodox approach of the Shia, and the offshoots of Kharijism, Ahmadiyya, and Ismaili beliefs which not every Muslim recognizes. In addition, there is the Sufi tradition which opens Islam to a wide assortment of influences.

Fourth, it gives Muslims a sense of identity and belonging. As it is considered a "way of life" due to its minute regulations in areas such as food, liquor, and dress, it gives guidance to the uncertain. Reinforcing the psychological comfort of these certainties, the religion informs its members that they are part of a world-wide community — the umma or jumma.

Related to the above psychological aspects of the religion, Islam simultaneously offers comfort from both a macro and micro level. The prevalence of brotherhoods in both Africa and Europe (tariqa) allows members to feel part of a global order. At the same time, at the local level of the tariqa is attractive to individuals who crave belonging to a small intimate affinal group similar to a clan or tribe. Conversely, its hierarchical organization at the overall level is also compatible with those people who desire structure. Furthermore, the idea of an all-knowing supreme leader whether it is an imam at the mosque or a shaikh/sheik in a local brotherhood (Sufi or otherwise) also meets a felt need for inner security.

The devotional aspect of Sufism is its mystical union of the parishioner with the Almighty. The various stages of initiation (dikr) tied to attainment of a spiritual goal is compatible with traditional practices in Africa and Europe. Also attractive is the visit of tombs of saints which although incompatible with strictly orthodox observance is seen as a continuation with pre-existing Islamic practices and does represent an alternate Islamic tradition. The concept of a spiritual guide whether it is the imam of a mosque or of a sheik (teacher/master) in an order/brotherhood is in fact a universal factor in all belief systems — a figure who can be both to ancestors and the hereafter. The imam is the guardian of the sacred knowledge of the holy texts (of special importance to a non-literate congregation or a congregation which lacks knowledge of Arabic). The sheik can be a saint in waiting to be the object of veneration after pilgrimage to their tombs. This master can hold a moral spear

Part VIII: Conclusion 139

or even a political/military one. He also is the gatekeeper to esoteric sacred knowledge and meaning that is derived from mystical communication with Allah.

The two sides of Islam — rational knowledge of religious texts and their prescriptives including law codes is consonant with the search for order and stability in human nature; mystical devotion including praying with gesticulation and movement is attractive to the emotional side of people. The multi-dimensional nature of Islam in its various versions has an enduring appeal. This circumstance is unlikely to change in the near future. Islam is not monolithic and often assumes the coloration of the society in which it exists as has been seen in the countries examined in this study. In North Africa, in western Libya and Algeria, there has been an accommodation with Berber culture especially in the interior areas. In Mali and Nigeria in West Africa, Islam was re-imposed by the Fulani although it commingled with the indigenous Mande and Hausa peoples respectively. In East Africa, Islam arrived with traders associated with the Indian Ocean trade and initially was coastal and Swahili-centered. In the heterogeneous Caucasus, it spread gradually over a millennium and often arrived with the Sufis. It later assumed an anti-imperialist and anti-Russian character. In the Balkans, Islam arrived with the Ottomans and in part (at least until recently) reflects the characteristics of its original progenitors. In the western European countries studied, the traits of evolving Islam mirrors the traits of the largest ethnic Muslim group — North African in France, Pakistani in Great Britain, and Turkish in Germany. The challenge of globalization and modernization will test its age-old resilience.

Muslim societies face another challenge which is a response to globalization and modernization. This is the arrival of militant often violent forms of Islamic extremism. In very area that has been studied, with the exception of Albania, Azerbaijan, and Bosnia-Herzegovina at the moment, this form of violent Islam has arisen not only to confront civil society but also more establishmentarian moderate forms particularly since 1990. The new arrival can take various forms. It can take root from an indigenous movement such as Boko Haram in Nigeria, Al-Shabaab in Somalia, and the Emirate of the North Caucasus in Chechnya and Dagestan. It can be connected with Al-Qaeda such as AQIM or MUJAO in North Africa and W Africa. It can be indigenous at the outset, but supported by external forces such as the Saudi supported Wahhabi movement and the Egyptian-supported Salafi movement among Muslims in Western Europe and in Tanzania as well as Al-Qaeda. The sectarian challenge can be especially threatening when, as is the case of

Nigeria, and, to some extent, Libya where regional identification is at least as strong as national identity. In other cases, the Islamic forces can be better armed, better trained or more highly motivated as in the case of Mali, Somalia, and, formerly, Chechnya. Whether internal, external, or a combination of both, this new variant is part of the equation which must be met if a society is to balance future prospects with past heritage so as to function in the present.

ENDNOTES

Chapter 1

[1] Nehemiah Levitzion and Randall L. Pouwels, "Introduction," Levitzion and Pouwels (eds), *The History of Islam in Africa* (Athens, Ohio: University Press, 2000), pp. 1-20.

[2] Ibid.

[3] Ibid., Peter von Sivers, "Egypt and North Africa," in Levitzion and Pouwels, op.cit., pp. 21-37.

[4] Ibid.

[5] Vernon O. Egger, *A History of the Muslim World to 1405* (Upper Saddle River, N.J.: Pearson/Prentice Hall, 2004), pp. 37-38, 145-146, 164-165, 250.

[6] Ibid., pp. 41-42.

[7] Ibid., pp. 94-96, 154-159.

[8] Levitzion and Pouwels, pp. 25-26.

[9] Egger, pp. 162-169.

[10] Ibid., pp. 123-127.

[11] Ibid., p. 250.

[12] Ivor Wilks. "The Juula and the Expansion of Islam into the Forest," in Levitzion, pp. 93-110.

[13] Ibid.

[14] Jay Spaulding, "Pre-Colonial Islam in the Eastern Sudan," in Levitzion, pp. 117-130.

[15] Vernon O. Egger, *A History of the Muslim World Since 1260* (Upper Saddle River, N.J.: Pearson/Prentice Hall, 2008), pp. 130-135.

[16] Ibid., pp. 279-285.

[17] J. Spencer Trimingham, *A History of Islam in West Africa* (London: Oxford University Press, 1970), pp. 153, 157-159.

[18] David Robinson, *Muslim Societies in African History* (Cambridge: Cambridge University Press, 2004), pp. 185-187.

[19] Ibid, pp. 139-153.

[20] See chapter on Nigeria.

[21] C.M. Kusimba, *The Rise and Fall of Swahili States* (London: Sage, 1999), pp. 19-39.

[22] Ibid.

[23] Thomas H. Wilson, *City-States of the Swahili Coast* (New York: Rosen, 1998), pp. 29-37.

[24] Kusimba, pp. 117-145.

[25] Ibid.

[26] Wilson, pp. 39-47.

[27] http://www.riseofislam.com/europe_and_islam_02.html (accessed on December 7, 2013)

[28] Ibid.

[29] http://www.bbc.co.uk/religion/religions/islam/history/earlyrise_1.shtml (accessed on December 8, 2013)

[30] Ibid.

[31] http://www.historyofjihad.org/france.html?bl=culture (accessed on December 9, 2013).

[32] Ibid.

[33] http://www.islamawareness.net/Europe/Russia/russian_article004.html (accessed on December 7, 2013).

[34] Ibid.

[35] Ibid

[36] See later chapter on Azerbaijan.

[37] Ibid.

[38] www.islamicpluralism.org/.../the-heritage-of-ottoman-islam-in-the-balkans.

[39] http://english.islammessage.com/ArticleDetails.aspx?articleId=815, Nexhat Ibrahim, "How Islam made its way into the Balkan Peninsula." (retrieved December 1, 2013).

[40] Ibid.

[41] Ibid.

[42] See later chapter on Albania.

[43] http://lcweb2.loc.gov/frd/cs/cshome.html: Library of Congress, Country Studies: Kosovo.

[44] Ibid, Country Studies: Macedonia.

[45] Pew Forum, http://www.pewforum.org/2011/01/27/the-future-of-the-global-muslim-population.

[45] Ibid.

[46] Ibid.

[47] Ibid.

[48] Ibid.

[49] Ibid.

[50] See chapters on the Caucasus.

[51] See chapters on the European Diaspora.

[52] http://rt.com/news/islam-challenges-secular-turkey-861/

Chapter 2

[1] http://lcweb2.loc.gov/frd/cs/cshome.html: Library of Congress, Country Studies: Algeria.

[2] Ibid.

[3] Ibid.

[4] Ibid.

[5] Vernon O. Egger, *A History of the Muslim World to 1405* (Upper Saddle River: Pearson, Prentice Hall, 2004), p. 172.

[6] Ibid., pp. 182-186.

[7] Ibid., pp.186-188.

[8] See Jamil M. Abun-Nasr, *A History of the Maghrib in the Islamic Period*, 3rd ed.(Cambridge: Cambridge University Press, 1987) for the early period.

Endnotes

143

[9] Vernon O. Egger, *A History of the Muslim World since 1260* (Upper Saddle River: Pearson, Prentice Hall, 2008), pp. 124-127.

[10] Ibid., p. 298.

[11] Library of Congress, Algeria: "Colonization and Military Control," op.cit.

[12] http://www.cfr.org/world/islamism-algeria-struggle-between-hope-agony/ p7335 Council on Foreign Relations Paper, Ray Takegh, "Islamism in Algeria: A Struggle between Hope and Agony", pp. 1-8.

[13] John Entelis, *Islam, Democracy, and the State in North Africa*, (Bloomington, Indiana: University of Indiana Press, 1997), p.63ff.

[14] John Entelis and Philip Naylor, *State and Society in Algeria*, (Boulder: University of Colorado Press, 1995), pp. 50-59.

[15] John Esposito, *Political Islam: Revolution, Radicalism, or Reform* (Boulder: University of Colorado Press, 1997), passm.

[16] Takegh, pp. 9-10.

[17] Ibid.

[18] Ibid., pp. 12-13.

[19] Ibid., pp. 13-14.

[20] Ibid., pp. 15-17.

[21] http://www.theguardian.com/world/2008/aug/20/algeria. alqaida (retrieved on November 20, 2013).

[22] https://thewasat.wordpress.com/author/matzahwarrior/ "of mergers, Mujao...." by Andrew Lebovich, August 23,2013 (retrieved on November 21, 2013).

[23] http://www.al-monitor.com/pulse/security/2013/08/north-africa-terrorism-groups-al-qaeda-merge.html (retrieved on November 22, 2013)

[24] http://www.al-monitor.com/pulse/security/2013/08/north-africa-terrorism-groups-al-qaeda-merge.html (retrieved on November 23,2013)

[25] Takegh, pp. 14-15.

[26] Ibid.

[27] Ibid.

Chapter 3

[1] http://lcweb2.loc.gov/frd/cs/cshome.html: Library of Congress, Country Studies: Libya. Information for notes 1 through 3 on West Africa can be found in http://education.national geographic.com/education/encyclopedia/africa-physical-geography/ ?ar_a=1 (retrieved on October 3, 2014)

[2] Vernon O. Egger, *A History of the Muslim World to 1405* (Upper Saddle River: Pearson, Prentice Hall, 2004), p. 41.

[3] Vernon O. Egger, *A History of the Muslim World since 1260* (Upper Saddle River: Pearson, Prentice Hall, 2008), pp. 125-129.

[4] Ibid., pp. 298-299.

[5] Ibid., p. 320.

[6] Country Studies: Libya op.cit.

[7] http://berkleycenter.georgetown.edu/resources/countries/libya (retrieved on November 24, 2013).

[8] Ibid.

9 Ibid.

10 Country Studies: Libya.

11 Egger, Muslim World Since 1260, pp. 382-384.

12 http://www.everyculture.com/Ja-Ma/Libya.html (retrieved November 26, 2013)

13 Ibid.

14 See chapters on Mali and Nigeria.

15 Knut Viker, "Sufi Brotherhoods in Africa," pp. 456-457 in Levitzion and Pouwels (eds), *The History of Islam in Africa* (Athens, Ohio: University Press, 2000).

16 Ibid.

17 Ibid.

18 http://www.mathaba.net/info/islam.htm Islam in Libya (retrieved November 26, 2013).

19 Ibid.

20 Ibid.

21 Ibid.

22 http://www.mideastafrica.foreignpolicy.com/posts/2012/11/02/introducing_the_libyan_ muslim_brotherhood (retrieved on November 28, 2013).

23 David H.Kirkpatrick, "Election Results in Libya Break an Islamic Wave," http://nytimes.com 2012/07/09 (retrieved November 29, 2013).

24 http://www.thedailybeast.com/articles/2012/09/12/what-is-ansar-al-sharia.html (retrieved on November 30, 2013).

25 Ibid.

26 David H. Kirkpatrick, "A Deadly Mix," http://www.nytimes.com/ projects/2013/benghazi/# /?chapt=0 (retrieved on December 28, 2013).

Chapter 4

1 J. Spencer Trimingham, *A History of Islam in West Africa* (London: Oxford University Press, 1970), pp, 34-104.

Notes for the first three notes are also found under http://education. National geographic.com /education/encyclopedia/africa-physical-geography/?ar_a=1 (retrieved on October 3,2013)

2 Ibid.

3 Ibid., pp. 8-34.

4 Consult Nehemiah Levitzion, "Islam in the Bilad-al-Sudan to 1800,"in Levitzion and Pouwels (eds), *The History of Islam in Africa* (Athens-Ohio: University Press, 2000).

5 Ibid.

6 Ivor Wilks. "The Juula and the Expansion of Islam into the Forest," in Levitzion, pp. 93-110.

7 Trimingham, pp. 154-171.

8 Ibid.

9 Ibid., pp. 60-83.

10 Ibid., pp.141-154,

11 Wilks, op. cit.

12 Jay Spaulding, "Pre-Colonial Islam in the Eastern Sudan,"in Levitzion, pp. 117-130.

13 Knut Viker, "Sufi Brotherhoods in Africa," pp. 441-468 in Levitzion and Pouwels (eds), *The History of Islam in Africa* (Athens, Ohio: University Press, 2000).

14 David Robinson, *Muslim Societies in African History* (Cambridge: Cambridge University Press, 2004), pp. 139-152.

Endnotes   145

[15] Vernon O. Egger, *A History of the Muslim World since 1260* (Upper Saddle River: Pearson, Prentice Hall, 2008), pp. 281-283.

[16] Trimingham, pp. 177-180.

[17] Ibid., pp, 181-185.

[18] Ibid., pp. 181-192.

[19] Ibid, pp. 171-181.

[20] see Jean Louis Triaud, "Islam in Africa under French Colonial Rule," in " Levitzion and Pouwels (eds), *The History of Islam in Africa* (Athens, Ohio: University Press, 2000), pp. 169-188.

[21] Consult Lansine Kaba, " Islam in West Africa...," in Levitzion and Pouwels, op.cit.pp. 190-193.

[22] Ibid., pp. 195-196.

[23] Ibid, pp. 201-202.

[24] Ibid., pp. 203-204.

[25] http://www.bbc.com/news/world-africa-24587491 retrieved on December 6, 2013.

[26] Ibid.

[27] Ibid.

[28] See https://www.fas.org/sgp/crs/row/R42664.pdf (Congressional Research report on Crisis in Mali — retrieved January 20, 2014).

[29] Ibid.

[30] Ibid.

[31] Ibid.

Chapter 5

[1] SJ Hogben and A.H.M. Kirke-Greene, *The Emirates of Northern Nigeria* (London: Oxford University Press, 1966), pp. 89-98.

[2] Ibid., pp. 307-313.

[3] Ibid., pp. 313-316.

[4] Ibid.

[5] The CIA World Factbook has especially relevant information, see http:/www.cia/gov/library /publications/factbook/geos/ng/html

[6] Ibid.

[7] http://www.gowestafrica.org/peoplegroups/ (retrieved December 11, 2013).

[8] J. Spencer Trimingham, *A History of Islam in West Africa* (London: Oxford University Press, 1970), pp. 186-189.

[9] Hogben and Kirk-Greene, pp. 116-130.

[10] Ibid., pp. 151-164.

[11] David Robinson, *Muslim Societies in African History* (Cambridge: Cambridge University Press, 2004), pp. 142-151.

[12] Hogben and Kirk-Greene, pp. 145-230.

[13] Ibid., pp. 360-420.

[14] Ibid., pp. 302-342.

[15] Knut Viker, "Sufi Brotherhoods in Africa," pp. 446-447 in Levitzion and Pouwels (eds), *The History of Islam in Africa* (Athens, Ohio: University Press, 2000).

16 David Robinson, "Revolutions in Western Sudan," pp. 131-152 in Knut Viker, "Sufi Brotherhoods in Africa," pp. 441-468 in Levitzion and Pouwels (eds), *The History of Islam in Africa* (Athens, Ohio: University Press, 2000).

17 William S.F. Miles, "Religious Pluralism in Northern Nigeria," pp. 209-226 in Levitzion and Pouwels (eds), *The History of Islam in Africa* (Athens, Ohio: University Press, 2000).

18 Ibid.

19 Ibid.

20 Ibid, pp. 218-221.

21 Ibid, pp. 223-225.

22 Ibid, pp. 215-219.

23 David Laitin, "The Sharia Debate and the Origins of the Second Republic," Journal of Modern African Studies, Vol. 20, pp. 411-430.

24 Miles, pp. 219-220.

25 http://www.bbc.com/news/world-africa-12192152 (retrieved December 2,2013)

26 http://www.bbc.com/news/world-africa-12192152 (retrieved December 2, 2013).

27 www.workersliberty.org/story/2013/08/07/tragedy-biafran-war (retrieved December 2, 2013)

28 Miles, p. 218.

29 Ibid., p. 219.

30 See http://www.bbc.com/news/world-africa-13951696 (retrieved December 3, 2013). It summarizes events from 2002 to 2013 in Nigeria.

31 Ibid.

32 Ibid.

33 Ibid.

34 Ibid.

35 Ibid.

36 http://www.cfr.org/nigeria/boko-haram/p25739 This site covers a Council on Foreign Relations report on the Bolo Haram and its offshoots. (retrieved on December 4, 2013).

37 Ibid.

38 See the article on Mend at nai.diva-portal.org/smash/get/diva2: 280470/FULLTEXT01.pdf (retrieved on December 5, 2013).

Chapter 6

1 C.M. Kusimba, *The Rise and Fall of Swahili States* (London: Sage, 1999), p. 2.

2 Ibid., p.3 passim.

3 Thomas H. Wilson, *City-States of the Swahili Coast* (New York: Rosen, 1998), pp. 29-30.

4 http://lcweb2.loc.gov/frd/cs/cshome.html: Library of Congress, Country Studies: Somalia.

5 Ibid.

6 Ibid.

7 ews.google.com/newspapers?nid=266&dat=19850615&id=5vsrAAAAIBAJ&sjid=gG0FAAAA IBAJ&pg=2508,6505397 (Associated Press article on "Mad Mullah.")

8 http://www.africalap.blogspot.com/.../sufis-and-jihadists-in-somalia-and-east.html (retrieved on December 9, 2013).

9 atheism.about.com/library/FAQs/islam/.../bl_SomaliaIslamTenets.htm (retrieved on December 10, 2013).

Endnotes 147

[10] www.mongabay.com/.../somalia-persecution_of_the_majeerteen.html (also covered in the Library of Congress, Country Studies: Somalia) (retrieved on December 11,2012).

[11] Martin N. Murphy, Somalia: *The New Barbary: Piracy and Islam in the Horn of Africa* (New York: Columbia University Press, 2011), pp. 7-16.

[12] Ibid., pp. 39-47.

[13] Kenneth J. Menkhaus, " Somalia and Somaliland: Terrorism, Political Islam, and State Collapse" in Robert I. Rotberg (ed.) *Battling Terrorism on the Horn of Africa*, (Washington, D.C: Brookings Institution Press, 2004), p.23.

[14] Ioan Lewis, *Understanding Somalia and Somaliland* (London: Hurst, 2008), pp. 35-50,

[15] Murphy, pp. 165-167.

[16] Ibid., pp. 18-70.

[17] Ibid., pp. 75-80.

[18] Ibid., pp. 81-90.

[19] www.bbc.com/news/world-africa-24587491 (retrieved on December 12, 2013).

[20] Ibid.

[21] Ibid.

[22] Murphy, pp. 39-43.

Chapter 7

[1] J. Spencer Trimingham, *Islam in East Africa* (London: Edinburgh House Press, 1962), pp. 30-39.

[2] Randall L. Pouwels, " The East African Coast, c. 780 to 1900 c.e.," pp. 251-253 in Levitzion and Pouwels (eds), *The History of Islam in Africa* (Athens, Ohio: University Press, 2000).

[3] C.M. Kusimba, *The Rise and Fall of Swahili States* (London: Sage, 1999), chapter 5.

[4] Ibid.

[5] Ibid.

[6] Thomas H. Wilson, *City-States of the Swahili Coast* (New York: Rosen, 1998), pp. 29-33.

[7] Ibid., pp. 34-36.

[8] Pouwels, op.cit., pp. 261-266.

[9] David C. Sperling, " The Coastal Hinterland and Interior of East Africa," pp. 273-276 in Levitzion and Pouwels (eds), *The History of Islam in Africa* (Athens, Ohio: University Press, 2000).

[10] Ibid., pp. 281-286.

[11] Ibid., pp. 286-290.

[12] Ibid., pp. 293-298.

[13] See, for example, CH Becker, "Materials for the Understanding of Islam in German East Africa," Tanzania Notes and Records,68, trans. B.G. Martin, pp.31-61.

[14] B. Brown, "Muslim Influence on Trade and Politics in the Lake Tanganyika Region," African Historical Studies, No. 4, 1971, pp.617-630.

[15] Sperling, pp. 274-278.

[16] Ibid.

[17] Abdin Chande, "Radicalism and Reform in East Africa," pp. 349-353in Levitzion and Pouwels (eds), *The History of Islam in Africa* (Athens, Ohio: University Press, 2000).

[18] Ibid., pp. 360-364.

[19] Ibid.

148 Norman C. Rothman

[20] Ibid.

[21] Consult Henry Bienen, Tanzania: *Party Transformation and Economic Development*, (Princeton: Princeton University Press, 1971), pp. 20-50.

[22] http://www.zanzinet.org/zanzibar/history/historia.html (retrieved on December 14, 2013).

[23] Ibid.

[24] Ibid.

[25] http://www.independent.co.uk/news/world/Africa. "Trouble in Paradise as Radical Islam grows in Zanzibar." p. 2.

[26] Ibid., p.3.

[27] Ibid.

[28] Ibid.

[29] Chande, op.cit., p. 364.

[30] Ibid.

[31] http://www.pewforum.org/2011/01/27/the-future-of-the-global-muslim-population (retrieved on December 15, 2013.

Chapter 8

[1] Gerald Robbins, *The Growth and Influence of Islam in the Nations of Asia and Central Asia.* (Philadelphia: Mason Crest Publishers, 2005), pp. 13-19.

[2] Ibid., pp. 27-31.

[3] Ibid., pp. 31-34.

[4] Ibid., p. 118.

[5] See CIA, The World Factbook at http://www.cia.gov/cia/publications/ factbook/geos/aj.html

[6] Anar Valiyev, "Azerbaijan: Islam in a post-Soviet Republic," Middle East Review of International Affairs, Vol. 9, no.4-December 22, 2005., p.1.

[7] Ibid., p.7.

[8] Ibid., p. 8.

[9] Raul Monika, "Islam in Post-Soviet Azerbaijan," in Archives des Sciences Social des Religions, Volume 115 (Summer 2001), p.113.

[10] Alec Rasizade, "Azerbaijan in Transition in the New Age of Democracy," Communist and Post-Communist Studies, Vol. 36, no. 3 (2003), pp. 342-343.

[11] Robbins, p. 55-57.

[12] Ibid., pp. 53-55; 85-87.

[13] Ibid., p.97.

[14] Arif Yusuvov, *Islam in Azerbaijan* (Baku: Zamani Press, 2004), passim.

[15] Svant Cornell, Politicization of Islam in http://www.silkwood studies/org/view/docs/silkroad papers/0610.Azei/pdf. P. 23 (accessed January 4, 2012).

[16] See http://azerb.com.

[17] Valiyev, p. 6.

[18] Ibid, pp. 7-11.

[19] See H. Kotecka,"Islamic and Ethnic Identities in Azerbaijan: Emerging Trends and Tensions: A Discussion Paper" (2006) found at http://www. osce.org/Baku/238094 (accessed January 5, 2012).

[20] Ibid.

[21] Robbins, pp. 74-75.

Endnotes 149

22 Consult http://www.bakusun.az:8101/index.html.

23 Ibid.

24 Robbins, pp. 83-84.

25 Ibid., see also the section on Chechnya.

26 Consult https://www.cia.gov/library/publications/the-world-factbook/geos/aj.html on Azerbaijan. See also following references.

27 http://www.bbc.com/news/world-europe-17043424 (retrieved on December 16, 2013).

28 Ibid.

29 Ibid.

Chapter 9

1 Robert Bruce Ware and Enver Kisriev, *Dagestan: Russian Hegemony and Islamic Resistance in the North Caucasus* (London: M.E. Sharpe, 2010), pp. 36-39.

2 Ibid., pp. 4-7.

3 Ibid.

4 See Michael Reynolds, "Myths and Mysticism: A Longitudinal Study Perspective on Islam and Conflict in the North Caucasus,"Middle Eastern Studies, Vol. 41, no. 1,(January 2005), pp. 31-54.

5 Hillary Pilkington and Galina Yamelianova, *Islam in Post-Soviet Russia* (London: Routledge, 2003), P.28; 47.

6 Ware and Kisriev, pp. 12, 20, 25.

7 Reynolds, pp. 33-34.

8 Pilkington and Yamelianova, p. 29 passim.

9 Ware and Kisriev, pp. 20-27.

10 Marie Bennigsen Broxup, "The Last Ghazavat: the 1920-21 Uprising" pp.112-145 in *The North Caucasus Barrier: The Russian Advance towards the Muslim World* (London: Hurst, 1992). See also Ware and Kisriev, p.30.

11 Alexandre A. Bennigsen, "Muslim Conservative Opposition to the Soviet Regime: The Sufi Brotherhoods in the North Caucasus," pp. 334-48; in Jeremy R.Azrael (ed,) *Soviet Nationality Policies and Practices* (New York: Praeger, 1978).

12 Ware and Kisriev pp. 29-31.

13 D. Hiro, *Between Marx and Muhammad* (London: Harper Collier, 1994), p. 32.

14 Pilkington and Yamelianova, pp. 50-59.

15 Ibid.

16 Ware and Kisriev, pp., 90-109.

17 Ibid., pp. 120-124.

18 Ibid., pp. 124-127.

19 See Yaacov Roi, *Islam in the Soviet Union*, (New York: Columbia University Press, 2000), Part V.

20 Ware and Kisriev, pp, 90, 101-103.

21 Pilkington and Yamelianova, pp.149-151.

22 Ibid.

23 Ibid.

24 See Robert Ware, et al., "Dagestan and Stability in the Caucasus," pp. 12-23 in Problems of Post-Communism, Vpl. 5-, no. 2 (March-April 2003).

[25] Ware and Kisriev, pp, 98-102.

[26] Ibid.

[27] Walter Comins-Richmond, "Legal Pluralism in the Northwest Caucasus: The Role of the Sharia Courts," in Religion, State, and Society, Vol. 32, March 1, 2004.

[28] Ibid.

[29] Pilkington and Yamelianova, pp. 150-152.

[30] Ibid.

[31] See next chapter.

[32] Consult, for example, Rajan Menon, "Russia's Quagmire: On Ending the Standoff in Chechnya," Boston Review (Summer 2004).

Chapter 10

[1] For background information, consult http://www.amazon.com/The-Chechens-Handbook-Caucasus-Peoples/dp/0415323282 (retrieved December 14)

[2] Yaacov Roi, *Islam in the Soviet Union*, (New York: Columbia University Press, 2000), pp. 90-92.

[3] Robert Bruce Ware and Enver Kisriev, *Dagestan: Russian Hegemony and Islamic Resistance in the North Caucasus* (London: M.E. Sharpe, 2010), p. 210, pp. 11-12, pp.20-25.

[4] Ibid., p. 26.

[5] Ibid.

[6] Richard Sakwa, " Introduction: Why Chechnya," pp. 1-21, in Chechnya: From Past to Future, Richard Sakwa (ed.) London: Anthem Press, 2005.

[7] Valentin Mikhailov, "Chechnya and Tartarstan: Differences in Search of an Explanation," pp. 43-66 in Sakwa, op.cit.

[8] Roi, pp. 303-304.

[9] See Marie Bennigsen Broxup, (ed) *The North Caucasus Barrier: The Russian Advance towards the Muslim World* (London: Hurst, 1992).

[10] Alexandre A. Bennigsen, " Muslim Conservative Opposition to the Soviet Regime: The Sufi Brotherhoods in the North Caucasus," pp. 334-48; in Jeremy R.Azrael (ed,) *Soviet Nationality Policies and Practices* (New York: Praeger, 1978).

[11] Anna Zelkina, "Islam and Politics in the North Caucasus," pp. 15-124 in Religion, State, and Society, Vol. 21, no. 1, 1995.

[12] Alexander Cherkasov and Dimitry Grushkin, pp. 131-156 in Sakwa, op.cit.

[13] Ibid.

[14] Tom de Waal, "Chechnya: The Breaking Point," pp. 181-198 in Sakwa, op.cit.

[15] Robert Bruce Ware and Enver Kisriev, *Dagestan: Russian Hegemony and Islamic Resistance in the North Caucasus* (London: M.E. Sharpe, 2010), p. 221-227.

[16] Ibid.

[17] Ibid.

[18] Pavel K. Baev, "Chechnya and the Russian Military: A War too Far," pp. 117-129 in Sakwa, op.cit.

[19] http://www.bbc.com/news/world-europe-18190473 (timeline) retrieved on December 16, 2013.

[20] Ibid.

[21] Ibid.

[22] videocast.nih.gov/summary.asp?Live=4679 –covers both the Moscow Theater and Beslan incidents. (retrieved on December 17, 2013)

Endnotes

151

23 http://usatoday30.usatoday.com/news/world/story/2012-03-21/chechnya-islamic-revival /5369 3048/1(retrieved on December 18, 2013)

24 Ibid.

25 Ibid.

Chapter 11

1 http://www.pewforum.org/2011/01/27/the-future-of-the-global-muslim-population/   (retrieved on December 19, 2013).

2 Ibid.

3 http://lcweb2.loc.gov/frd/cs/cshome.html: Library of Congress, Country Studies: Albania.

4 Ibid.

5 See www.balkaninsight.com/.../albanian-muslims-grapple-with-religious-identity (retrieved on December 19, 2013).

6 Ibid.

7 See www.da.mod.uk/colleges/arag/document-listings/.../08(09)MV.pdf (retrieved on December 19), paper on Albanian Islam.

8 Miranda Vickers,"Islam in Albania," *A paper for the Advanced Research and Assessment Group, Defence Academy* (September 8, 2009) "Introduction.".

9 Ibid., "Historical Background."

10 Ibid.

11 Ibid.

12 www.balkaninsight.com/.../albanian-muslims-grapple-with-religious-identity (retrieved on December 19, 2013).

13 https://www.weeklystandard.com/blogs/kosovo-radical-islamists-new-political-offensive_701 196.html?page=2

14 http://www.bbc.com/news/world-europe-17550407   (Macedonia   Profile)   (retrieved   on December 19,2013)

15 http://serbianna.com/analysis/archives/2043 (retrieved on December 20,2013)/

16 http://lcweb2.loc.gov/frd/cs/cshome.html: Library of Congress, Country Studies: Albania.

17 www.balkaninsight.com/.../albanian-muslims-grapple-with-religious-identity (retrieved December 20, 2013).

18 Vickers, "Recent Developments in the Albanian Religious Community"

19 Ibid.

20 Ibid.

21 Ibid.

22 Balkan Insight, op. cit.

23 Ibid.

24 Ibid.

25 Country Profiles: Albania, op. cit.

26 James Pettifer and Miranda Vickers, *The Albanian Question*, (London: Taurus, 2009), Chapter 16.

27 Ibid., Chapter 17.

28 Consult, The World Almanac of Islamism: Albania, Fetullah Gullen Movement.

29 Ibid.

30 Margaret Hasluk, "The Non-conformist Moslems of Albania," The Moslem World, Volume XV, 1925, pp. 392-393.

152 Norman C. Rothman

[31] Vickers, "Education."
[32] Ibid., "Conclusion."

Chapter 12

[1] Noel Malcolm, *Bosnia: A Short History* (New York: New York University Press, 1994), pp. 51-52.

[2] John Fine, *"The Various Faiths in the History of Bosnia: Middle Ages to the Present"* in Islam and Bosnia (Maya Shatzmiller, ed.), (Montreal: McGill University Press, 1996), pp. 1-5.

[3] Ibid., pp. 5-6.

[4] Malcolm, pp. 20-50.

[5] Thomas W. Arnold, The Preaching of Islam: A History of the Propagation of the Muslim Faith, (New York: Constable and Company, 1914), passim.

[6] Fine, pp. 6-7.

[7] Ibid, pp. 7-8.

[8] Ibid.

[9] F. Friedman, *The Bosnian Muslim: Denial of a Nation*, (New York City: Westview Press, 1996), pp. 18-50.

[10] Peter Sugar, Southeastern Europe under Ottoman Rule: 1354-1804, (Seattle: University of Washington, 1992) passim bid.

[11] Ibid.

[12] See Robert Okey, *"State, Church and Nation in the Serbo-Croat Speaking Lands of the Habsburg Monarchy, 1850–1914". Religion, State and Ethnic Groups.* (New York University Press, 1992)

[13] Fine, 9-10.

[13] Ibid., 10-12.

[14] Ibid., pp. 12-14. Consult Paul Moizes. Balkan Genocides: Holocaust and Ethnic Cleansing in the Twentieth Century. Lanham, Maryland: Rowman & Littlefield, 2011. p. 98-105.

[15] Ibid., p. 15.

[16] See M. Glenny, *The Fall of Yugoslavia: The Third Balkan War.* (New York: Penguin, 1992).

[17] See Bosnia war timeline at ews.bbc.co.uk/2/hi/europe/country_ profiles/1066981.stm (retrieved December 21, 2013).

[18] Consult http://www.eurac.edu/en/research/institutes/imr/Documents/ 13BosniaHerzegovina. pdf for settlement details (retrieved on December 21, 2013)

[19] See ww.icty.org/x/file/About/OTP/War_Demographics/en/bih_casualty_undercount_conf _ paper_100201.pdf for estimate of war losses. (retrieved on December 21, 2013)

[20] Tone Bringa, "Islam and the Quest for Identity in Post-Communist Bosnia-Herzegovina," pp. 24-33 in Shatzmiller, op.cit.

[21] See ww.akademie-rs.de/fileadmin/user.../071116_albasic_bosnianislam.pdf on the nature of Bosnian Islam (retrieved on December 21)

[22] http://www.bbc.com/news/world-europe-17212376 See general chronology of events. (retrieved on December 22, 2013).

[23] articles.chicagotribune.com/1996-09-08/news/9609080294_1_banja-luka-bosnian-serb-serb-authorities (retrieved on December 22, 2013) report on mixed marriages.

[24] articles.chicagotribune.com/1996-10-20/news/9610200198_1_bosnian-refugees-berlin-govern ment-bosnian-croats/2 for refugee crisis. (retrieved on December 22, 2013)

Endnotes

153

[25] http://www.washingtontimes.com/news/2011/nov/10/radical-islam-in-the-heart-of-europe/ (retrieved on December 22, 2013)

[26] Ibid

[27] Ibid.

[28] http://www.5pillarz.com/2013/07/31/the-rise-of-political-islam-in-eastern-Europe/ (retrieved on December 22)

[29] Ibid.

Chapter 13 (with Part VII introduction)

[1] http://www.pewforum.org/2011/01/27/the-future-of-the-global-muslim-population/ (retrieved on December 19, 2013).

[2] Ibid.

[3] Ibid.

[4] Ibid.

[5] Ibid.

[6] Ibid.

[7] http://www.gatestoneinstitute.org/2355/france-islam-overtaking-catholicism (retrieved on December 22, 2013)

[8] Alison Pargeter, *The New Frontiers of Islam*, (London: I. B. Tauris, 2008), pp. 83-89.

[9] Robert S. Leiken, *Europe's Angry Muslims*, (Oxford: Oxford University Press, 2012), pp. 38-40.

[10] Ibid, pp. 24-25.

[11] See www.thenewamerican.com/.../11347-french-muslims-overwhelming- supported-socialist (retrieved December 22, 2013)

[12] Jonathan Lawrence and Justin Vaisse, "Understanding Urban Riots in France," New Europe Review, December 1, 2005. See also Leiken, p. 37.

[13] Charles Krautheimer, " What the Uprising Generation Wants, Time, November 13, 2005,

[14] Leiken, pp. 39-46.

[15] Ibid.

[16] John R. Bowen, *Why The French Don't Like Headscarfs: Islam, the State, and Public Space* (Princeton: Princeton University Press, 2007), p. 83.

[17] Ibid., pp. 100-125.

[18] Ibid.

[19] Lawrence and Vaisse, p. 226; Leiken, p.21.

[20] Leiken, p. 22.

[21] Ibid., p. 32.

[22] Consult, for example, John Carreyrou, "Culture Clash: Muslim Groups May Gain Strength from French Riots,...," Wall Street Journal, November 7, 2005.

Chapter 14

[1] See http://www.pewforum.org/2011/01/27/the-future-of-the-global-muslim-population/(retrieved on December 19, 2013).

154 Norman C. Rothman

[2] See Pew Global Attitudes Project (Washington D.C.: Pew Research Center, 2006) p. 3ff.

[3] Ibid.

[4] Robert S. Leiken, *Europe's Angry Muslims*, (Oxford: Oxford University Press, 2012), p. 67; p. 82.

[5] Ibid., pp. 68-71; pp. 83-86.

[6] Philip Lewis, *Islamic Britain: Religion, Politics and Identity Among British Muslims* (London: Tauris, 1994), p.79.

[7] Giles Kepel, *Jihad: The Trail of Political Islam* (Cambridge: Harvard University Press, 2002), pp. 37-39.

[8] Christian Joppke, "Limits of Immigration Policy: Britain and Her Muslims," Journal of Ethnic and Migration Studies, Vol. 35. No. 3 (March 2009), p. 455.

[9] Randall Hansen, *"Citizenship and Immigration in Post-war Britain"*, (Oxford: Oxford University Press, 2000), p. 16.

[10] Ibid., pp. 120-121.

[11] Ibid., pp. 123-124.

[12] Ibid.

[13] Christian Joppke, "Asylum and State Sovereignty: A Comparison of the United States, Germany, and Britain," Comparative Political Studies, Volume 30, No. 3, (1997), p. 101.

[14] Quintan Wiktorowicz, *Radical Islam Rising: Muslim Extremism in the West* (New York: Rowman and Littlefield, 2005), p.7.

[15] Leiken, p. 153.

[16] Ibid, pp. 160-166.

[17] Ibid., p. 159; pp. 175-177.

[18] Lewis, p. 25.

[19] See Roger Ballard, "The South Asian Presence in Britain and its Transnational Connections," pp. 26-27 in Blukhu Parekh et.al., *Culture and Economy in the Indian Diaspora* (London: Routledge, 2003).

[20] Ibid., p. 27.

[21] Leiken, pp. 180-185.

[22] Ibid.

[23] Ibid., pp. 185-187.

[24] Ibid., pp. 157-159.

[25] http://gawker.com/terror-in-london-soldier-hacked-apart-by-machete-wield-509321352 (retrieved on December 23, 2013).

[26] http://www.gatestoneinstitute.org/4112/islamization-britain (retrieved on December 23, 2013)

[27] http://www.gatestoneinstitute.org/4205/britain-immigration#comment_ submit (retrieved December 23,2013).

Chapter 15

[1] Robert S. Leiken, *Europe's Angry Muslims*, (Oxford: Oxford University Press, 2012), p. 239.

[2] Ibid., pp. 240-242.

[3] Olivier Roy, *Globalized Islam* (New York: Columbia University Press, 2004), p, 26 and passim.

[4] Consult "Ialam and Identity in Germany," International Crisis Group, Europe Report 181, March 2007.

[5] Leiken, pp. 243-245.

Endnotes

155

[6] http://www.thelocal.de/20111010/38113 (on education of Turkish Children) (retrieved on December 24, 2013)

[7] See Imre Karacs," Germany's Turkish Children Sink into the Underclass," Independent(UK) November 12, 2000.

[8] Christopher Caldwell, "Where Every Generation is First Generation," New York Times Magazine, May 27, 2007.

[9] Claus Mueller, "Integrating Turkish Communities: A German Dilemma," Population Research and Policy Review" Volume 25 December, 2006.

[10] Leiker, pp, 246-247,

[11] Ibid, p. 247.

[12] Guido Steinberg, " A Turkish al-Qaeda: The Islamic Jihad Union and the Internalization of Uzbek Jihadism," Strategic Insights, July, 2008.

[13] See http://www.worldpoliticsreview.com/author.asps. Available September 17, 2007 (retrieved December 24, 2013).

[14] See http://pewglobal.org/2006/07/06/muslims in europe (retrieved on December 24, 2013).

[15] consult http://www..guardian.co.uk/world/2010/mat/04/islamic-jihad-union-bomn-plot (retrieved December 24, 2913).

[16] Leiken, pp. 248-249.

BIBLIOGRAPHY OF BOOKS AND ARTICLES

Chapter 1

Bulliet, Richard. *The Camel and the West.* Cambridge: Harvard University Press. 1975.

Collins, Roger. *The Arab Conquest of Spain.* Oxford: Basil Blackwell, 1989.

Egger, Vernon O. *A History of the Muslim World to 1450.* Upper Saddle River, NJ: Pearson/Prentice Hall, 2004.

_____ . *A History of the Muslim World Since 1260.* Upper Saddle River, NJ: Pearson, Prentice Hall, 2008.

Kusimba, C.M. *The Rise and Fall of the Swahili States.* London: Sage, 1999.

Levitzion, Nehemiah and Randall L. Pouwels, "Introduction." In Nehemiah Levitzion and Randall L. Pouwels, eds., *The History of Islam in Africa.* Athens, Ohio: University Press, 2000.

Robinson, David. *Muslim Societies in African History.* Cambridge: Cambridge University Press, 2004.

Spaulding, Jay. "Pre-Colonial Islam in the Eastern Sudan." In Nehemiah Levitzion and Randall L Pouwels, eds., *The History of Islam in Africa.* Athens, Ohio: University Press, 2000.

Trimingham, J. Spencer. *A History of Islam in West Africa.* London: Oxford University Press, 1970.

Von Sivers, Peter. "Egypt and North Africa." In Nehemiah Levitzion and Randall L. Pouwels, eds., *The History of Islam in Africa.* Athens, Ohio: University Press, 1970.

Wasserstein, David J. *The Caliphate in the West.* New York: Oxford University Press, 1993.

158   Norman C. Rothman

Wilks, Ivor. "The Juula and the Expansion of Islam into the Forest." In
   Nehemiah Levitzion and Randall L. Pouwels, eds., *The History of Islam in
   Africa*. Athens, Ohio: University Press, 1970.
Wilson, Thomas H. *City States of the Swahili Coast*. New York: Rosen, 1998.

Chapter 2

Abun-Nasr, Jamil M. *A History of the Maghrib in the Islamic Period*.
   Cambridge: Cambridge University Press, 1987.
Brett, Michael. *The Rise of the Fatimids*. Leiden: Brill, 2001.
_____ and Elizabeth Fentriss. *The Berbers*. Oxford: Blackwell. 1996.
Bulliet, Richard. *Conversion to Islam*. Cambridge, Mass: Harvard University
   Press, 1979.
Egger, Vernon O. See bibliography in Chapter 1.
Entellis, John. *Islam, Democracy, and the State in North Africa*. Bloomington,
   Indiana: University of Indiana Press, 1997.
_____ and Phillip Naylor. *State and Society in Algeria*. Boulder: University
   of Colorado Press, 1995.
Esposito, John. *Political Islam: Revolution, Radicalism, or Reform*. Boulder:
   University of Colorado Press, 1997.
Julien, Charles-Andre. *History of North Africa*. Translated by John Petrie.
   New York: Praeger, 1970.
Powell, James M., ed. *Muslims Under Latin Rule, 1100-1300*. Princeton, NJ:
   Princeton University Press, 1970.

Chapter 3

Abun-Nasr. See chapter 2 bibliography.
Baldick. Julian. *Mystical Islam: An Introduction to Sufism*. London: Taurus,
   1989.
Brett and Fentriss. See Chapter 2 bibliography.
Bulliet, See chapter 2 bibliography.
Burgat, F. and William Dowell. *The Islamic Movement in North Africa*.
   Austin, University of Texas Press, 1993.
Egger. See Chapter 1 bibliography.
Entellis. See Chapter 2 bibliography.

Bibliography of Books and Articles   159

Fitzgerald, David. "Election Results in Libya Break an Islamic Wave." In http://nytimes.com 2012/07/09

———. "A Deadly Mix." In http://www.nytimes.com/projects/2013/benghazi/#/?chapter=0

Julien. See Chapter 2 bibliography.

Martin, Bradford G. *Muslim Brotherhoods in Nineteenth-century Africa.* Cambridge: Cambridge University Press, 1978.

Peters, Emrys L. *The Bedouin of Cyrenica.* Cambridge: Cambridge University Press, 1990.

Trimingham, J. Spencer. *The Sufi Orders in Islam.* London: Oxford University Press, 1971.

Viker, Knut S. *Sufi and Scholar on the Desert Edge: Muhammad b. Ali al-Sanussi and His Brotherhood.* Evanston: Northwestern University Press, 1995.

———. *Sources for Sanusi Studies.* Bergen: Centre for Middle Eastern Studies, 1996.

———. "Sufi Brotherhoods in Africa" in Nehemiah Levitzion and Randall. ouwels.eds *The History of Islam in Africa.* Athens: Ohio University Press, 2000.

Chapter 4

Abun Nasr, Jamil. *The Tijaniyya.* Oxford: Oxford University Press, 1965.

Curtin, Philip. "The Jihads of West Africa: Early Relations and Linkages." *Journal of African History,* Volume 2, pp. 11-24, 1971/

Egger, Vernon O. See bibliography in Chapter 1.

Hanson, John. *Migration, Jihad, and Muslim Authority in West Africa.* Bloomington: Indiana University Press, 1971.

Harrison, Chris. *France and Islam in West Africa(1860-1960).* Cambridge: Cambridge University Press, 1988.

Kaba, Lansine. "Islam in West Africa: Radicalism and the New Ethic of Disagreement" in Levitzion and Pouwels. See bibliography in Chapter 3.

Kano, Moustapha and David Robinson. *The Islamic Regime of Futa Toro.* East Lansing: African Studies Center, Michigan State University, 1984.

Levitzion, Nehimiah. "Islam on the Bilad-al-Sudan to 1800" In Levitzion and Pouwels. See bibliography in chapter 3.

Robinson, David. *Muslim Societies in African History.* See bibliography in chapter 1.

160 Norman C. Rothman

Rodney, Walter. "Jihad and Social Revolution in Futa Jalon in the Eighteenth Century." In *Journal of the Historical Society of Nigeria,* 4, 269-284, 1968.

Spaulding, Jay. See Bibliography in chapter one.

Triaud, Jean Louis. "Islam in Africa under French Colonial Rule." In Levitzion and Pouwels. See Bibliography in chapter one.

Trimingham, J. Spencer. *A History of Islam in West Africa.* See bibliography in chapter one for the full citation.

Viker, Kurt. "Sufi Brotherhoods in Africa." See bibliography in chapter one.

Wilks, Ivor. See bibliography under chapter one.

Chapter 5

Anderson, Hilary. "Two Branches of Islam Clashing in Nigeria." *New York Times,* October 10, 1996.

Clarke, Peter. *West Africa and Islam.* London: Edward Arnold, 1982.

Crowder, Michael. *A Short History of Nigeria.* New York: Praeger, 1962.

Gilliland, Dean. *African Religion Meets Islam: Religious Change in Northern Nigeria.* Lanham, Md: Iniversity Press, 1986.

Hiskett, Mervyn. *The Sword of Truth: The Life and Times of Shehu Usman dan Fodio.* Oxford: Oxford University Press, 1973.

———. "The Maitatsine Riots in Kano." *Journal of Religion in Africa* 17 209-225.

Hogben, SJ and A.H.M Kirk-Greene. *The Emirates of Northern Nigeria.* London: Oxford University Press, 1966.

Ibrahim, Jibrin. " Religion and Political Turbulence in Nigeria." *Journal of Modern African Studies,* 1991, 29, 115-136

Laitin, David. "The Sharia Debate and the Origins of the Second Republic." *Journal of Modern African Studies,* 1982, 20, 411-430.

Miles, William S.F. "Religious Pluralism in Northern Nigeria." In Levitzion and Pouwels(eds), *The History of Islam in Africa.* Athens, Ohio: Ohio University Press, 2000, pp. 229-226.

Robinson, David. "Revolutions in Western Sudan." In Levitzion and Pouwels (eds), *The History of Islam in Africa.* Athens, Ohio: Ohio University Press, 2000, pp. 131-152.

Chapter 6

Ahmad, Ismail I. and Reginald Herbold Green. " The Heritage of War and State Collapse in Somalia and Somaliland." *Third World Quarterly,* Vol. 20, No, 1, February 1999, pp. 161-121.

Chalk, Peter. *Non-Military Security and Global Order: The Impact of Extremism, Violence and Chaos on National and International Security.* London: Macmillan, 2002.

Le Sage, Andre. " Prospects for Al Ithihad & Islamic Radicalism on Somalia," *Review of African Political Economy,* Vol. 28, Issue 89, 2001.

Lewis, Ioan. *Understanding Somalia and Somaliland.* London: Hurst, 2008.

_____ *Blood and Bone: the Call of Kinship in Somali Society.* Lawrenceville, NJ: The Red Sea Press, 1994.

Little, Peter D. *Somalia: Economy without a State.* Bloomington. IN: Indiana University Press, 2003.

Menkhaus, Ken. "Somalia and Somaliland: Terrorism, Political Islam, and State Collapse." In Robert I. Rotberg (ed.), *Battling Terrorism in the Horn of Africa.* Washington, DC: Brookings Institution Press, 2005.

_____ . *Somalia: State Collapse and the Threat of Terrorism.* Oxford: Oxford University Press, 2004.

Murray, Martin F. *Somalia: The New Barbary? Piracy and Islam in the Horn of Africa.* New York: Columbia University Press, 2011.

Terdman, Moshe. "Somalia at War — Between Radical Islam and Tribal Politics." *Research Paper No. 2.* Tel Aviv: Tel Aviv University, the S. Daniel Abraham Center for International and Regional studies, March 2008.

Chapter 7

Balda, J.L. "Swahili Islam: Continuity and Revival." *Encounter* (March 193-194), pp. 1-29.

Becker, CH. "Materials for the Understanding of Islam in German East Africa." In *Tanzania Notes and Records,* 68, trans. B.G. Martin, 31-61, 1968.

Bienen, Henry. *Tanzania: Party Transformation and Economic Development.* Princeton: Princeton University Press, 1971.

Brown, B. "Muslim Influence on Trade and Politics in the Lake Tanganyika Region." *African Historical Studies,* no. 4, 1971. pp. 617-630.

Chande, Abdin. *Islam, Ulamaa, and Community Development in Tanzania, East Africa.* San Francisco: Austin & Lawler, 1998.

————. "Radicalism and Reform in East Africa." In Levitzion and Pouwels(eds), *The History of Islam in Africa* Athens, Ohio: Ohio University Press, 2000.

Iliffe, John. *A Modern History of Tanganyika.* Cambridge: Cambridge University Press, 1979.

Nimitz, A. H. *Islam and Politics in East Africa, the Sufi Order in Tanzania.* Minneapolis: University of Minnesota Press, 1980.

Pouwels, Randall. " The East African Coast, c. 780 to 1900 C.E." In Levitzion and Pouwels (eds.), *The History of Islam in Africa.* Athens, Ohio: Ohio University Press, 2000.

Sperling, David C. " The Coastal Hinterland and Interior of East Africa." On Levitzion and Pouwels (eds), *The History of Islam,* Athens, Ohio: Ohio University Press, 2000.

Trimingham, J. Spencer. *Islam in East Africa.* London: Edinburgh House Press, 1962.

Chapter 8

Alstadt, Audrey. *The Azerbaijani Turks: Power and Identity Under Russian Rule.* Stanford: Hoover Institution Press, 1992.

Cornell, Svant. *Politicization of Islam.* Accessed on January 4, 2012 from http://www.silkwood.

Kotecka, H. (2006). "Islamic and Ethnic Identities in Azerbaijan: Emerging Trends and Tensions — A discussion Paper. Accessed on January 8, 2012. http://www.osce.org/Baku/238094.

Leeuw, Charles van der. *Azerbaijan: A Quest for Identity.* New York: St. Martin's Press, 1989.

Monika, Raul. "Islam in Post-Soviet Azerbaijan," in *Archives des Sciences Social des Religions,* Volume 115 (Summer 2001).

Rasizade, Alec "Azerbaijan in Transition in the New Age of Democracy," *Communist and Post-Communist Studies,* Vol. 36, no. 3, 2003. pp.342-346.

Robbins, Gerald *The Growth and Influence of Islam In Asia and Central Asia: Azerbaijan.* Philadelphia: Mason Crest Publishers, 2005.

Valiyev, Anar. "Azerbaijan: Islam in a post-Soviet Republic."*Middle East Review of International Affairs,* Vol. 9, no. 4, 2005.

Yusouvov, Arif. *Islam in Azerbaijan.* Baku: Zamani Press, 2004.

Zenkovsky, Serge A. *Pan-Turkism and Islam in Russia.* Cambridge, Mass: Harvard University Press, 1960.

Chapter 9

Bennigsen, Alexandre. "Muslin Conservative Opposition to the Soviet Regime: The Sufi Brotherhoods in the North Caucasus." In Jeremy R. Azrael (ed.), *Soviet Nationality Polices and Practices.* New York: Praeger, 1978.

Broxup, Marie Bennigsen. " The Last Ghazavat: the 1920-21 Uprising." In Marie Bennigsen Broxup (ed). *The North Caucasus Barrier: The Russian Advance towards the Muslim World.* London: Hurst, 1992.

Hiro, D. *Between Marx and Muhammad.* London: Harper Collier, 1994.

Pilkington, Hillary and Galina Yamelianova. *Islam on Post-Soviet Russia.* London: Routledge, 2003.

Reynolds, Michael. "Myths and Mysticism: A Longitudinal Study of the Perspective on Islam and Conflict in the North Caucasus," in *Middle Eastern Studies,* Vol 42, No. 1 (January 2005), pp. 31-54.

Richmond, Walter Comins. "Legal Pluralism in the Northwest Caucasus: The Rise of the Sharia Courts," in *Religion, State, and Society,* Vol. 32, March 1, 2004.

Roi, Yaacov. *Islam in the Soviet Union,* New York: Columbia University Press, 2000.

_____. *The USSR and the Muslim World.* London: Allen & Unwin, 1984.

Ware, Robert Bruce and Enver Kisriev, *Dagestan: Russia Hegeminy and Islamic Resistance in the North Caucasus.* London: M. E. Sharpe, 2010.

_____ . "Political Stability in Dagestan: Ethnic Parity and Religious Polarization." In *Problem of Post-Communism* 47, no. 2 (March-April 2000).

Chapter 10

Baev, Pavel. "Chechnya and the Russian Military: A War too Far?" In *Chechnya: From Past to Future,* Richard Sakwa(ed,). London: Anthem Press, 2005.

Benningsen, Alexandre and S. Enders Wimbush, *Muslim National Communism in the Soviet Union.* Chicago: University of Chicago Press 1979.

_____. *Muslims of the Soviet Empire: A Guide.* London: Hurst, 1986.

_____. *Myths and Commissars: Sufosm in the Soviet Union.* London: Hurst, 1985.

De Waal, Tom. "Chechnya: The Breaking Point." In *Chechnya: From Past to Future,* Richard Sakwa(ed,). London: Anthem Press, 2005.

Mikhailov, Valentin, "Chechnya and Tatarstan: Differences in Search of an Explanation." In *Chechnya: From Past to Future,* Richard Sakwa(ed,). London: Anthem Press, 2005.

Sakwa, Richard. " Introduction: Why Chechnya." In *Chechnya: From Past to Future,* Richard Sakwa(ed,). London: Anthem Press, 2005.

Trimingham, J. Spencer. *The Sufi Orders in Islam.* Oxford: Oxford University Press, 1973.

Wilhelmsen, Julie. "Between a Rock and a Hard Place: The Islamisation pf the Chechen Separatist Movement," *Europe — Asia Studies,* Vol. 57, No. 1, January 2005, pp, 35-59.

Zelkina, Anna. "Islam and Politics in the North Caucasus," *Religion, State, and Society,* Vol. 21, No, 1, 1993, pp. 115-124,

Chapter 11

Biberaj, Elez. *Albania in Transition,* Westview CT: Westview Press, 1998.

Booth, K. (ed). *The Kosovo Tragedy.* London: Cass, 2001.

Hasluk, Margaret, "The non-conformists Moslems of Albania," *The Moslem World,* Vol. XV, 1925, pp. 392-393.

Judah, Tim. *The Kosovo War and Revenge.* London: Oxford University Press, 2000.

Paskal, Milo. *Greater Albania — Between Fiction and Reality.* Tirana: privately printed, 2001.

Pettifer, James (ed). *The new Macedonian Question.* London: Palgrave, 2001.

_____ . "Balkan asylum seekers — time for a new approach?" Migration Watch Paper, 2003 retrieved from www.migrationwatch.org

_____ and Miranda Vickers. *The Albanian Question: Reshaping the Balkans.* London: Taurus, 2009.

Vickers, Miranda. "Islam in Albania." A paper for the Advanced Research and assessment Group, Defense Academy (September 8, 2009)

Bibliography of Books and Articles   165

_____ . "Pan-Albanianism — how big a threat to Balkan Stability?" International Crisis Group, February 4, 2004 retrieved from www.crisisgroup.org

Chapter 12

Arnold, Thomas. *The Preaching of Islam: A History of the Propagation of the Muslim Faith,* New York: Constable and Company, 1914.

Bringa, Tone. "Islam and the Quest for Identity in Post-Communist Bosnia-Hercegovina. In *Islam and Bosnia* (Maya Shatzmiller, ed.). Montreal: McGill University Press. 1996.

Fine, John. "The Various Faiths in the History of Bosnia: Middle Ages to the Present." In *Islam and Bosnia* (Maya Shatzmiller, ed.). Montreal: McGill University Press, 1996.

Friedman. F. *The Bosnian Muslim: Denial of a Nation.* New York City: Westview Press, 1996.

Glenny, Michael. *The Fall of Yugoslavia: The Third Balkan War.* New Yotk: Penguin, 1992.

Malcolm, Noel. *Bosnia: A Short History,* New York: New York University Press, 1994.

Moizes, Paul. *Balkan Genocides: Holocaust and Ethnic Cleansing in the Twentieth Century* Lanham, Maryland: Rowman & Littlefield, 2011.

Okey, Robert. " State., Church, and Nation in the Serbo-Croat Speaking Lands of the Habsburg Monarchy, 1850-1914)." In *Religion, State, and Ethnic Groups* (Robert Okey, ed,). New York: New York University Press, 1992.

Shatzmiller, Maya (ed.). *Islam and Bosnia.* Montreal: McGill University Press, 1996.

Sugar, Peter. *Southeastern Europe under Ottoman Rule: 1354-1804.* Seattle: University Press, 1994.

Chapters 13, 14, 15 with Part VII

Ballard, Roger. "The South Asian Presence in Britain and its Transnational Connections." In Blukhu Parekh et al., *Culture and Economy in the Indian Diaspora,* London: Routledge, 2003.

Bowen, John R. *Why the French Don't Like Headscarfs: Islam, the State, and Public Space.* Princeton: Princeton University Press, 2007.

Caldwell, Caldwell. "Where Every Generation is First Generation." In *New York Times Magazine*, May 27, 2007.

Carreyrou, John. "Culture Clash: Muslim Groups may Gain Strength fom French Riots..." *Wall Street Journal*, November 7, 2005.

Hansen, Randall. *Citizenship and Immigration in Post-war Britain*. Oxford: Oxford University Press, 2000,

Joppke, Christian. "Limits of Immigration Policy: Britain and Her Muslims," *Journal of Ethnic and Migration Studies*, Vol. 35, No. 3 (March 2009).

_____ . "Asylum and State Sovereignty: A Comparison of the United States, Germany, and Britain," *Comparative Political Studies*, Volume 30, No. 3, 1997.

Karacs, Imre. " Germany's Turkish Children Sink into the Underclass," *Independent (UK)*, November 12, 2000.

Kepel, Giles. *Jihad: The Trail of Political Islam*. Cambridge: Harvard University Press, 2000.

Krautheimer, Charles. "What the Uprising Generation Wants," *Time*, November 13, 2005.

"Lawrence, Jonathan and Justin Vaise. "Understanding Urban Riots in France," *New Europe Review*, December 1, 2005.

Leiken, Robert S. *Europe's Angry Muslims*. Oxford: Oxford University Press, 2012.

Lewis, Philip. *Islamic Britain: Religion, Politics and Identity Among British Muslims*. London: Tauris, 1994.

Mueller, Claus. "Integrating Turkish Communities: A German Dilemma," *Population Research and {olicy Review*, Volume 25, December 2006.

Pargeter, Alison. *The New Frontiers of Islam*. London: Tauris, 2008.

Roy, Olivier. *Globalized Islam*. New York: Columbia University Press, 2004.

Steinberg, Guido. "A Turkish al-Qaeda: The Islamic Jihad Union and the Internationalization of Uzbek Jihadism," *Strategic Insights*, July 2008.

Wiktorowicz, Quintan. *Radical Islam Rising: Muslim Extremism in the West*. New York: Rowman and Littlefield, 2005.

GLOSSARY

Chapter 1

Gezira — This is the region in north-central Sudan where the blue and white Nile meet to form the main Nile-an historic cultural transmission area.

Adulis — ancient port on the Red Sea which proved to be an entry point for Islam into what is now Ethiopia and Eritrea.

Maghrib — the area of North Africa between central Libya and the Atlantic Ocean.

Bani Hillal — Arab nomadic tribe who helped to Arabize and Islamize Egypt and adjoining parts of Libya in the 11th century.

Almoravids — Militant Berber Muslim order which conquered much of North African and Spain as well as destroy the West African empire of Ghana between the mid-11th and mid-12th centuries..

Almohads — Successor order to the Almoravids which ruled much of the same area from approximately the latter part of the 12th to the latter part of the 13th centuries.

Berbers — indigenous inhabitants of North Africa.

Fatimids — North African Shia dynasty which established a third caliphate in Egypt from the mid-10th to early 12th centuries.

Al-Azhar — Famous Islamic center of learning established in Cairo in the mid-11th century.

Banu Sulaym — another Arab tribe who helped to Arabize and Islamize western Libya, Tunisia, and part of Algeria.

Sudanic belt --- grassland area between the Sahara and rain forest belts from which Islam spread south.

Mali --- fabled predominantly Muslim empire between 1235 and 1470 famed for its wealth.

Timbukti — city in northern Mali known not only for its wealth, but also for its learning.

Sankore — Famous university in Timbuktu.

Mande — African group mostly from Mali whose members spread Islam along trade routes to the south in West Africa.

Swahili — an African culture with Arabic and middle eastern admixture that dominated the coastal region from Somalia to Mozambique and was celebrated for its wealth as a middleman between interior Africa and the Indian Ocean littoral; it helped to Islamize much of the East African coast from the horn of Africa southward.

Al-andalus — modern day Andalusia but originally was the name for most of the Iberian peninsula when it was under Muslim control especially from the 8th to the 13th century.

Cordova — the most famous of the Muslim principalities because of its ealth and learning; it became a separate caliphate when a survivor from the former Umayyad dynasty fled to Spain and formed a separate state in the mid-eighth century to the early 12th century.

Moriscos — Spanish Muslims who captured their faith in secret to some extent until their expulsion in the eraly 1600;s.

Granada — the last Muslim state in Spain to fall to the Christians in 1492.

Tours (or Poitiers) — historic battle in 732 which halted the Muslim advance into France.

Kazan — Tatar Muslim state in the north Volga/Ural region which lasted several centuries before falling to Tsar Ivan the terrible in the 17th century.

Astrakhan — the southern counterpart to Kazan in terms of religion, location, and fate.

Caucasus — mountain range between Europe and the Middle East which was penetrated in the south (Azerbaijan) and north (Dagestan) by Islam over the course of a millennium.

Ottoman Empire — the Turkish empire which controlled much of Southeastern Europe and the Balkans for approximately 5 centuries until 1804-1912 and helped influence many communities of Christians to Islam. Among the converts were Slavic peoples particularly Bosnians and Illyrian peoples especially Albanians/

Barbary pirates — pirates from Morocco, Algeria, Tunis, and Tripoli who raide much of coastal western Europe for slaves and loot and held ships for ransom until the early 1800"s.

Glossary 169

Chapter 2

Bey or dey — title of appointed ruler of Algiers under Ottoman rule.

Sanhaja –one of two Berber confederations in Algeria and adjoining areas.

Zenata — the other major Berber confederation in the western Maghrib.

Ab-al-Quadir — leader of Islamic resistance to French rule between 1839 and 1843.

National Liberation Front (FLN) — Guerilla group which fought for Algerian Independence between 1954 qnd 1962 and has been the ruling group since then.

Al-Quijan — moderate Islamic opposition groups in the early post-independence period which emphasized Islamic elements to be added to education.

Al-Irshal — another moderate Islamic group which Muslim elements added to social and economic activities in independent Algeria.

Islamic Salvation Front (FLS) — Islamic group which arose in the 1980's in opposition to secular policies of the Algerian government.

GIA or Armed Islamic Group — extremist wing of the FLS which arose after the 1991/1992 elections were cancelled when it appeared that the government might lose and engaged in a sanguinary uprising in the nineteen nineties which ultimately took approximate 150,000 lives.

The Salafist Group for Peace and Contentment or GSPC — the militant Islamic group which replaced the GIA in armed opposition to the government between 1999 and 2004.

Al-Qaeda in the Maghrib or AQIM — the militant Islamic group which has taken the lead in terrorist activities since 2004. It is active not only in Algeria but also in other North African states as well as adjoining West African states.

Quadariyya — global Sufi order which continues to exercise influence in Algeria.

Chapter 3

Cyrenaica — Eastern section of Libya which has been a local center of Islamic feeling in the country particularly in the cities of Benghazi and Derna.

Tripolitania — the Northwest and most populous section of Libya whose culture has always been associated with the Maghrib.

Fezzan — the desert or semi-desert central part of Libya that has traditionally beena center of Islamic feeling.

Karamanli — local dynasty which ruled both eastern and western Libya before the Turks took directly over in 1835.

Sanusiyya or Sanussi — Islamic brotherhood in North and West Africa whose center of gravity was in Cyrenica and Fezzan.

Omar-al-Mukhtiar –or "lion of the desert" — led a Muslim-based resistance to Italian colonialism for over two decades.

Tuaregs — east Maghribi Berbers who are active in Libya,

Toubou — the other major Maghribi Berber confederation in Libya.

Zawiya — Arabic term for a lodge in which Sufi live or visit.

Idris I — ruler of Libya between 1951 and 1969 whose rule was based on his descent from the founder of the Senussi/Sanusiyya order.

Moammar Khaddafi — dictator of Libya between 1969 and 2011 who tried to use Islam as a support for his rule.

Green Book — book attributed to Khadaffi which tried to modernize Islam.

National Forces Party — secular movement contending for power in contemporary Libya.

Ansar-al-Sharia — most militant of current Islamic movements which is identified with violent incidents in eastern Libya especially its largest city of Benghazi.

Benghazi — second city of Libya and located in Cyrenaica which also gained prominence as a center for violent incidences especially the murder of 4 Americans including the ambassador to Libya in September 2012.

Chapter 4

Dyula — Muslim traders from Mali who brought their religion with them to the forest region of West Africa.

Seku Ahmadu — Also known as Ahmadu Lobo. He founded an Islamic reformist state along the middle Niger in the early19th century.

Maliki — The Islamic law code prevalent in much of West Africa.

Al-Hajj Omar — Another Fulani Islamic reformer and cleric who adhered to the Tijaniyya order and established a large state on both the Niger and Senegal rivers.

Tijaniyya — a newer religious order which vied with the Quadiriyya order for influence in both Borth Africa and West Africa.

Glossary

171

Samori Toure — African leader who established a huge empire between Lake Chad and the Atlantic Ocean, and resisted French colonialism between 1882 and 1898,

Modibo Keita — First president of independent Mali who was considered anti-Muslim and ruled between 1960 and 1968.

Muslim Association for Unity and Progress — moderate Islamic group which attempted a consensus for all Muslims between 1970 and 2010.

Ansar Dine — Berber opposition group in northern Mali.

Maktar Belnakti — leader of Muslim opposition groups in north Mali in 2012-13 and founder of such groups as Masked Men and Signed in Blood.

Mujao. — or movement for monotheism and jihad which became the pre-eminent Islam opposition group in North Mali and is/was affiliated with Aqim.

Azawad — the proposed Berber Muslim state which would include northern Mali and adjacent Berber areas.

Chapter 5

Hausa — Largest ethnic group in West Africa, it dominates northern Nigeria and is significant in surrounding countries; it is the largest Muslim group in West Africa.

Bornu(Bornu) — historic Islamic state now located in Northeastern Nigeria.

Kano — largest city in Northern Nigeria whose records go back a millennium.

Katsina — most devoutly Muslim city in northern Nigeria; as was the case for Kano it gained its initial importance as a southern terminus of the trans-Saharan trade.

Fulani — pastoral nomadic group who led the Islamic revolutions in the 18th and 19th centuries/

Uthman dan Fodio — Muslim cleric who overthrew the existing somewhat backsliding Islamic cities in northern Nigeria (1804-1810) to establish a more orthodox state at Sokoto. Ultimately, his revolution affected neighboring countries through Hausa and Fulani populations.

Indirect Rule — the system established by Lord Lugard which allowed local rulers including Muslim ones to run their own affairs during colonial times.

Igbo — Non-Muslim group in southeast Nigeria which attempted secession after massacres by Muslims in the North.

Biafran war- conflict caused by attempted secession by the southeast between 1967 and 1970 which ultimately may have taken 1,000,000 lives.

Maitatsine — Islamic reformer whose followers rioted in the early 1980's, and who perished in a riot in Kano.

Al-zakzady — would-be successor to Maitatsine who was ultimately arrested and imprisoned.

Yoruba — southwestern Nigerians who are mostly non-Muslims.

MEND — revolutionary group in southeastern Nigeria who want a greater share of oil profits and recently have resorted to piracy.

Boko Haram- Islamic extremist group which has become active over the past decade and been responsible for the loss of tens of thousands of lives throughout Nigeria,

Ansaru — The most radical branch of Boko Haram and reportedly affiliated with AQIM.

Chapter 6

Adat — Medieval Muslim state in the Ethiopia/Somalia region.

Hawiye — Major Somali clan located in south and central Somalia some of whose members are involved in extremist Muslim groups.

Puntland — secessionist state in north central Somalia connected with the Darood clan (along with the Hawiye clan the most influential Somali clan) whose shores are the scene of the greatest piracy off the coast of Somalia.

Somaliland –secessionist north Somali state which corresponds with British Somaliland and is dominated by the Isaak clan (also present in Djbouti, the former French Somaliland).

Ajurram Confederation — first historical state that was both Somali and Muslim.

Mogadishu — originally a Swahili trading city now the capital of the country and the scene of the infamous Black Hawk Down incident.

Salihiyya — prominent Somali brotherhood.

Tarika/tariqa — generic term for Islamic brotherhoods.

Sayyid Muhammad — better known in history as the "Mad Mullah of Somaliland" who resisted European colonialism between 1898 and 1920.

Siad Barre — Socialist who ruled Somalia between 1969 and 1991.

Habir Gedir Ayr — Hawiye sub-clan prominent in factional disputes.

AIAI — first prominent militant Islamic group after the disintegration of Somalia in 1991.

Islamic Courts Union — Militant Muslim group prominent between 2000 and 2006 in government which arose out of traditional Islamic courts,

Al-Shabaab — Islamic terrorist group which has dominated south and central Somalia in recent years and has raided both Ethiopia and Kenya. It is affiliated with Al-Qaeda.

Chapter 7

Zanj — the ancient name for the central Swahili coast which corresponds to the present-day coast of Tanzania.

Kilwa — Swahili city in southern Tanzania which became the predominant Swahili city-state in the period 1100-1500 largely through its middleman position between the gold producing areas of Central Africa and the Indian Ocean.

Omani dynasty — Muscat-base family which established a trading network in eat-central Africa from Zanzibar.

Zanzibar and Pemba — Islands off Tanzania whose cinnamon and cloves plantation were the key driver of a vast slave trading network between 1840 and 1890.

Shafi'i — school of Islamic law prominent in mainland Tanzania.

Tanganyika African National Union (TANU)- largest political party in Tanaganyika until a name change in the nineties.

Julius Nyerere — leader of Tanzania from 1964 to 1987.

All Muslim National Union of Tanganyika or Amnut — Muslim opposition party to TANU in late colonial period.

Dawa — Muslim opposition group after independence.

Tanzania — new name after union of mainland Tanganyika and island of Zanzibar.

Muslim Students Union — current Islamic movement.

Bakwata — government backed Muslim group (Council of Muslim Organizations).

Warsha — most influential non-government Muslim group.

ZNP — Zanzibar National Party — political organ of Arab and South Asian groups in Zanzibar — ruled briefly until overthrown by African majority in 1964.

Bismullah — Muslim organization formed in Pemba in the "eighties."

Uamsho — Current political Muslim movement in Zanzibar which advocates secession of Zanzibar frim Tanzania.

Chapter 8

Albania — the ancient name for what is today Azerbaijan.

Aliyev — leader of Azerbaijan until his death in 2003.

Ashura — Shia holiday commemorating the death of Hussein in 680 C.E.

Azeri — an ethnic group divided between Iran (about 70% of the group) and an independent country (30%) in the southern Caucasus.

Baku — capital of Azerbaijan.

Caucasus Mountains — area which separates Europe from Asia and which is the location for the republic of Azerbaijan.

Cyrillic Alphabet — The alphabet adopted and discarded by the Azeri in an attempt to forge links with Europe. It was replaced by Latin.

Eid — the final day of Ramadan or breaking the fast.

Islamic (ist) Party of Azerbaijan — Islamic party backed by Iran which has been outlawed,

Law of Freedom of Religion — law passed in the early 1990's that restored all religious property taken during the Soviet period.

Muharran — traditional holiday nominally Islamic that involves self-flagellation) which many Azeri consider their most important holiday in Islam.

Nagorno-Karabakh — area inhabited by Armenians/Azeri located outside the borders of Armenia which has now been occupied by Armenia.

Novroz — literally "new birth," this holiday which is a national holiday that dates before Islam, is celebrated on the vernal equinox, and is the most popular holiday in Azerbaijan.

Pan-Turkism — a movement which seeks to unite all Turkic-speakers from Azerbaijan, Turkey, and Central Asia.

Salafists — a radical Islamic organization which originated from Egypt, and which is anti-Turkic and has been very active in missionary work and in the building of mosques. Its activities are closely monitored by the government.

Shirk — a derogatory term loosely translated as anti-Islamic that refers to religion when expressed through nationalism as not following true religion.

Spiritual Board of the Transcaucasus — the supreme religious authority in the state with headquarters in Baku and with a Shia chair and Sunni vice-chair.

Glossary

175

Chapter 9

Avars — largest of Dagestan's 41 ethnic groups.

Nasqshbandiyya — global Sufi order prominent in Dagestan.

Murids — followers of sheiks/shaykhs who are the heads of the brotherhoods or lodges of which they are members.

Imam Shamil — Muslim leader of revolt against Russians between 1831 and 1859.

Maktars — Dagestani equivalent of Koranic schools (elementary schools).

Shamil Basaev — Chechen Muslim warlord whose incursion into Dagestan in August/September 1999 led to a Russian crackdown in both Dagestan and Chechnya.

Habib Abid Al Rahman — also known as El Khattab, this Saudi cleric trained extremist Muslim guerillas in Chechnya and participated in the Dagestani incursion.

The Spiritual Directorate of Muslims of Dagestan or DUMD –This is the officially supported Muslim organization which has accrued a great deal of power over the past decade.

Islamic Party of Reform — A party which unsuccessfully attempted to bridge the gap berween moderates and extremists in the 'nineties.

Bagautdin Kebedov — Dagestani radical who attempted to form an Islamic enclave and went on to found the Islamic Emirate of Dagestan.

Islamic Emirate of the North Caucasus — The current premier organization for Islamic terrorism in the North Caucasus and beyond the limits of Dagestan.

Chapter 10

Vedeno — town in Chechnya which has been a center of Islamic militancy over the past century.

Murid Movement — Islamic resistance movement in the 19th century.

Vainakh — ethnic group which includes the Chechens and related groups such as the Ingush.

Dzhokhar Dudayev — Chechen leader who declared Chechen independenbce and was killed in 1996 during the first unsuccessful Russian invasion in 1996.

176   Norman C. Rothman

Aslam Mashkadov — second Chechen president (between 1996 and 200o) between 1996 and 2000 who became progressively more zealously Muslim.

Salman Radaev — Chechen warlord who espoused Muslim fundamentalism.

Grozny — Chechen capital which was leveled especially during the second successful Russian invasion of 2000.

Akhmat Kadyyrov — Chechen cleric placed in charge of Chechnya after 2000 by the Russians who was killed in 2003.

Ramzan Kadyrov — son of the former who was placed in charge by the Russians in 2007 where he remains today as a Russian protégé.

Beslan incident — the most notorious of terrorist incidents outside of Chechnya and Dagestan in which Chechen and Ingush rebels took over 1100 people mostly children at a school as hostage and ultimately by the time that they were killed at least 334 people most of them children had died.

Chapter 11

Bektashi _Sufi sect aligned with Shiite beliefs that is tolerant of Christianity and traditional beliefs and is a symbol of Albanian identity.

Kaprouku — Albanian family that rose to prominence as successive gramd viziers of the Ottoman Empire in the 17th century.

Pan-Illyrianism — Movement to unite all Albanians in the Balkans.

Justice Party — Pro-Muslim party in Kosovo.

Chams — Albanian Muslims living in northwest Greece.

Dyanat — Turkish Department of Muslim Affairs which has become a large donor to Albania.

Muslim Albanian Community — official organization for Albania Muslims.

Preservo — Albanian populated region of Southwest Serbia (also known as East Kosovo).

Fethullen Gullen — founder of movement which combines Islam with science. This Turkish group operates many schools in Muslim countries including Albania.

SEMA — religious foundation of Gulen which operates 5 out of 7 Madrasahs or religious high schools.

Enver Hoxha — Communist dictator of Albania (1945-1985) who suppressed religion.

Glossary 177

Sanjak of Novi Pazar — area between Serbia and Montenegro where many Albanians reside.

Macedonia — country with a large percentage of Albanians mostly but not entirely Muslim.

Hanbali — religious law code which most Albanian Muslims follow.

Chapter 12

Bogomils — heretical group of Christians who were persecuted and subsequently converted to Islam after Ottoman conquest.

Bosniak — name given to Bosnian Muslims.

Ustashe — Fascist regime in Croatia which also ruled Bosnia over WWII and was responsible for the deaths of hundreds of thousands of Serbs, Jews, and Gypsies.

Slobodan Milosevec –Serbian leader in the late eighties and the nineties who pursued a Greater Serbia at the expense of Bosnia and Bosnian Muslims.

Ethnic cleansing — a term which came to describe expulsion of groups especially of Muslims in Bosnia by mostly but not entirely Serbs.

Sarajevo-Bosnian capital (also the site of the assassination of Archduke Ferdinand which set off WWI) which suffered wholesale bombardment of its civilian population by Serbs and reached such a stage that NATO and the US eventually intervened.

Banka Luka — largest city in northern Bosnia ethnically cleansed of its Muslim majority population by Serbs.

Goradje — largest city in eastern Bosnia ethnically cleansed of its Muslim majority population by Serbs.

Srebrenica — the scene of the most notorious atrocity in the Bosnian war where over 8,000 Muslim boys and men were massacred.

Dayton accords –Agreement in 1996 which ended the fighting and established two separate states in one confederation.

Muslim-Croat Federation is one of the post-war components which contain 63% of the remaining population and 51% of its territory.

Serb Republic — This is the other post-war component of present-day Serbia.

Herzegovina — the southern quarter of Bosnia divided into a Moslem/Croat west and a Serb east.

Chapters 13, 14 and 15

Banlieu — French suburbs which are relatively short of amenities and have become ghettos for mostly Muslim North and West African immigrants.

Security urban zones — Muslim occupied urban areas where French law enforcement is sporadic and often non-existent.

No-go zones — colloquial term for the above term.

Muslim Brotherhood — organization which seeks political power for Muslims and had its origins in Egypt; it is active in both France and the United Kingdom.

World Muslim League — International branch of the Muslim Brotherhood especially active in France and the United Kingdom.

French Union of Islamic Organization-French branch of the Muslim Brotherhood especially active in France and supported by Qatar.

Headscarf controversy — or hijab controversy — the banning of this apparel worn by Muslim women in state-run public schools touched off acrimony for two decades.

Londonistan — pejorative term given to London by French security agents after they learned that a terrorist group had planned a wave if assassinations and bombings from London and also from the circumstance that in the nineties abd early 2000's hosted a large number of terrorist groups and radical preachers or imams. Some areas such as East London (and also other cities such as Leeds, Bradford, and Manchester) had areas where, as in France, government officials rarely ventured.

Lords of Londonistan — name given to the radical preachers.

Abu Qatada — a preacher designated by the UN Security Council as "al-Qaeda's spiritual ambassador to Europe."

Abu Hamza — preacher at London's most radical mosque — Finsbury Park.

Abdullah el Feisal –Preacher and Jamaica preacher who tutored the shoe bomber, the underwear bomber and the "twentieth hijacker" on 9/1.

Omar Bakri — Preacher who established a terrorist railroad network for training in Pakistan for bombers.

GIA –Algerian jihadi group that planned bombings from London.

HT or Party of Liberation (also active on Central Asia). This group is influential in both Britain and Germany and seeks Muslim governance.

Covenant of Security — now somewhat discarded doctrine which allowed extremists to organize and agitate as long as Britain was not harmed.

Islamic Movement of Uzbekistan (IMU) — Central Asian group also active in Germany.

Glossary

TJ (Tabligh Jama'at) — Islamic missionary group active in Europe.

Islamic Jihad Union — offshoot of the IMU in Germany.

Guestworker program — Labor recruitment Program which ultimately brought many Turkish Muslims to Germany.

Sauerland plot — a jihadi plot to kill at least 150 American soldiers in Germany.

Salafis, — Islamic fundamentalist branch that cites the life of the Prophet and his companions (salafis) as models for a religious life.

Wahhabis — a fundamentalist branch of Islam that ties Islamic dominance to the elimination any impurities such as shrines and holy men.

AUTHOR'S CONTACT INFORMATION

Professor Norman C. Rothman, Ph.D.
Department of History,
University of Maryland University College
E-mail: ncrothman@aol.com

INDEX

#

20th century, 17, 36, 99
9/11, 128, 129, 134

A

Abkhazia, 24, 25
abolition, 53, 55, 72
Abraham, 157
access, 90, 135
accommodation, 25, 45, 46, 53, 105, 118, 139
adaptation, 38
adjustment, 118
Afghanistan, 114, 129, 134
Africa, vii, ix, 13, 14, 15, 16, 17, 18, 19, 22, 23, 24, 26, 27, 29, 30, 33, 34, 35, 37, 41, 43, 45, 46, 49, 51, 52, 59, 61, 62, 63, 69, 71, 76, 111, 114, 117, 123, 127, 137, 138, 139, 141, 142, 143, 144, 145, 146, 147, 153, 154, 155, 156, 157, 158, 163,164, 166, 167, 169
age, 20, 48, 49, 62, 119, 126, 139
aggression, 63, 112, 113
aging population, 23
Akan, 44
Al Qaeda, 49
Albania, 22, 23, 99, 101, 102, 103, 104, 105, 106, 107, 108, 109, 110, 114, 115, 139, 142, 149, 150, 160, 170, 172

Algeria, vii, ix, 14, 15, 16, 20, 24, 29, 30, 31, 32, 33, 34, 36, 37, 49, 50, 117, 139, 142, 154, 163, 164, 165
alienation, 125, 134
alphabet, 170
al-Shabaab, 76
amalgam, 18
amputation, 38
ancestors, 61, 69, 88, 103, 138
ancient world, 61
anger, 88
annealing, 19
antagonism, 63
anthropology, ix
Arab countries, 33, 105
Arab world, 114
Arabian Peninsula, 13, 14, 18
Armenia, 25, 80, 82, 84, 170
Armenians, 81, 85, 170
arrest, 55, 83, 92
Asia, vii, 13, 21, 23, 61, 69, 71, 79, 80, 81, 89, 94, 97, 106, 114, 117, 134, 147, 158, 160, 170, 174
Asian countries, 104
assassination, 173
assessment, 160
assimilation, 25, 47, 118, 124, 125, 127
asylum, 160
athletes, 132
atmosphere, 91, 128
atrocities, 96, 113, 114
attitudes, 107

184 Index

Austria, 24, 111, 117, 118
authorities, 30, 31, 47, 53, 55, 64, 71, 81,
    91, 95, 102, 122, 127, 128, 150, 170
automobiles, 122
autonomy, 49, 109, 112
Azerbaijan, vii, ix, 21, 24, 25, 77, 79, 80,
    81, 82, 83, 84, 87, 95, 137, 139, 142,
    147, 158, 159, 164, 170

B

background information, 148
backlash, 118
Balkans, vii, 19, 22, 23, 24, 36, 77, 99, 103,
    107, 114, 139, 160, 164, 172
Balkars, 21
ban, 75, 123
Bangladesh, 125
base, 91, 166, 169
basic services, 130
Belgium, 24, 117, 118
belief systems, 138
beneficiaries, 72
benefits, 17, 30, 122
birth rate, 24, 104
Black Sea, 21, 79
blogs, 149
blood, 23, 25, 132
blueprint, 40
Bolshevik Revolution, 81, 88
bomb attack, 96
bones, 32
Bosnia, viii, ix, 22, 25, 99, 109, 110, 111,
    112, 113, 114, 115, 139, 150, 161, 173
Bosnia-Herzegovina, 99, 109, 139, 150
Bosnians, 23, 109, 110, 111, 113, 118, 164
breakdown, 36, 48
breeding, 121
Britain, ix, 53, 63, 74, 119, 125, 126, 127,
    128, 129, 130, 131, 132, 135, 139, 151,
    152, 161, 162, 174
Brittany, 125
brothers, 63
Buddhism, 138
Bulgaria, 22, 23, 24, 25, 80, 104, 105, 109

bureaucracy, 22, 53, 102, 110
Burkina Faso, 16, 41, 42, 44, 45, 53
Burundi, 18
businesses, 124

C

Cairo, 15, 19, 29, 35, 44, 64, 70, 163
Cameroon, 16, 18, 41, 44, 52, 53, 57
capitalism, 64
case studies, ix
cash, 106
Caspian Sea, 21, 79, 87
Catholic Church, 111
Catholics, 110, 111
caucasus, vii, ix, 20, 21, 24, 25, 77, 79, 82,
    87, 88, 89, 90, 92, 93, 94, 96, 117, 118,
    137, 139, 142, 148, 149, 159, 160, 164,
    170, 171
Central Asia, 21, 79, 81, 89, 91, 94, 97, 106,
    117, 134, 147, 158, 170, 174
Chad, 16, 17, 31, 36, 37, 41, 44, 47, 49, 51,
    167
challenges, 103, 125, 142
chaos, 39, 49, 55, 66, 94
charities, 104, 106
Chechens, 21, 84, 92, 93, 94, 95, 97, 148,
    171
Chechnya, vii, ix, 21, 25, 83, 88, 90, 91, 92,
    93, 94, 95, 96, 97, 139, 147, 148, 149,
    159, 160, 171, 172
Chicago, 160
children, 66, 95, 96, 124, 172
China, 19
Christianity, 13, 79, 103, 109, 126, 172
Christians, 14, 20, 22, 24, 54, 55, 56, 74, 75,
    80, 81, 105, 110, 111, 126, 164, 173
CIA, 144, 147
cities, 14, 16, 17, 19, 30, 31, 35, 36, 37, 39,
    43, 44, 45, 50, 52, 53, 61, 62, 66, 69, 70,
    71, 95, 110, 113, 118, 122, 134, 141,
    145, 146, 150, 154, 161, 165, 167, 174
citizens, 33, 117
citizenship, 25, 122, 127, 132, 135
civil liberties, 34

Index

civil servants, 32
civil society, 25, 26, 54, 139
Civil War, 88, 118
civilization, 47
classes, 17, 19, 44, 45, 52, 71, 110, 122
cleaning, 40, 133
cleavage, 49
climate, 127
clothing, 19, 70, 71
coastal region, 29, 164
collaboration, 47, 49
colleges, 32, 149
colonial rule, 31, 47
colonization, 64, 103
commerce, 44, 53, 69
commercial, 70, 97
communication, 139
community, 15, 24, 52, 63, 64, 66, 73, 81,
    99, 107, 112, 115, 125, 127, 130, 133,
    134, 138, 164
comparative religion, ix
compensation, 113
composition, 69
conference, 48, 90
configuration, 23
conflict, 15, 25, 29, 34, 55, 56, 64, 89, 94,
    95, 97, 104, 107, 114, 118, 168
Congo, 18, 19, 24, 61
congress, 142, 143, 145, 146, 149
consciousness, 57, 111
consensus, 48, 167
conspiracy, 105, 129
constitution, 82
construction, 44, 114
consumers, 84
consumption, 46
controversial, 55
conversion rate, 23, 61
cooperation, 72, 106
copper, 19, 61
corruption, 49, 52, 53, 55, 56, 57, 64, 85,
    90, 91, 92
cost, 33, 64, 65, 66, 95, 114
Council of Europe, 84
creep, 25, 55, 126

criminal activity, 95
critical thinking, 106
Croatia, 109, 110, 111, 112, 113, 173
cultural transmission, 13, 38, 41, 163
culture, ix, 13, 18, 19, 63, 70, 71, 72, 73, 76,
    80, 81, 83, 87, 93, 109, 115, 122, 132,
    137, 139, 142, 164, 165
currency, 41
curriculum, 48, 54, 111
Cyprus, 22, 25, 105

D

Dagestan, vii, ix, 21, 25, 82, 83, 87, 88, 89,
    90, 91, 92, 93, 95, 96, 139, 148, 149,
    159, 164, 171, 172
Darfur, 17
deaths, 56, 57, 173
decay, 91
deficiency, 133, 90
delegates, 90
Delta, 56
democracy, 135
demographic factors, 125
demonstrations, 75, 85, 122, 128
Denmark, 24, 118
deposits, 33, 84
deprivation, 23, 133
destruction, 44, 50, 57
detention, 73
discrimination, 25, 104, 123, 137
dissatisfaction, 32, 84
district courts, 88
diversity, 87
domestic policy, 84
dominance, 15, 65, 175
donations, 82
drawing, 25

E

earnings, 133
Easter, 103
economics, 94, 118, 127, 131

education, 29, 31, 32, 46, 48, 73, 74, 75, 89, 90, 104, 105, 106, 111, 128, 129, 133, 143, 144, 152, 165
educational career, 133
educational system, 84, 115
Egypt, 13, 14, 15, 18, 19, 29, 35, 40, 64, 82, 83, 102, 106, 107, 126, 141, 153, 163, 170, 174
election, 32, 56, 75, 94, 95, 104, 122, 134
electricity, 95
elementary school, 96, 171
Emancipation, 56
embassy, 76
emergency, 57
emigration, 25
employers, 126, 131
employment, 22, 95, 128, 131, 132, 133
encouragement, 23, 48
enemies, 65
energy, 84
enforcement, 121, 122, 174
England, 20, 128
environment, 37, 47, 105
equality, 48
Equatorial Guinea, 41
equilibrium, 76
equity, 32
Eritrea, 18, 63, 66, 163
ethics, 84
ethnic groups, 57, 73, 118, 171
ethnicity, 62, 79, 132
Europe, vii, viii, ix, 13, 19, 20, 21, 22, 23, 24, 25, 26, 30, 38, 41, 69, 77, 79, 80, 84, 103, 114, 115, 117, 118, 127, 131, 137, 138, 139, 142, 150, 151, 152, 160, 161, 162, 164, 170, 174, 175
European heritage, 25
European Studies, ix
European Union (EU), 24, 79, 84, 105, 118
evidence, 114
evolution, ix, 154
exaggeration, 17
exclusion, 15
executive branch, 123
exercise, 165

exile, 97
exports, 131
expulsion, 113, 164, 173
extinction, 114
extraction, 133
extremists, 50, 76, 91, 96, 123, 128, 129, 171, 174

F

Facebook, 40
factories, 31, 46, 71
faith, 22, 45, 80, 108, 111, 123, 164
families, 19, 71, 118, 131
famine, 66
farmers, 49, 69
fatwa, 129
federal government, 54
feelings, 48, 82, 114, 118
fertility, 119, 125
fertility rate, 119
fidelity, 82
financial, 30, 65, 66, 104, 107, 137
financial crisis, 104
financial support, 65, 105
folklore, 17, 81
food, 73, 138
footwear, 70
force, 26, 34, 50, 51, 87, 108
formation, 16, 38
foundations, 64, 104, 105
France, viii, ix, 14, 20, 24, 25, 31, 33, 53, 63, 109, 117, 119, 121, 122, 123, 124, 125, 126, 130, 131, 132, 135, 139, 151, 155, 162, 164, 174
freedom, 22, 64, 95, 110, 123
funding, 104
funds, 104

G

gangs, 56
gender equality, 48
genetics, 20

genocide, 109, 113
geography, 35, 48, 143, 144
Georgia, 24, 25, 80, 82
Georgians, 93
Germany, viii, ix, 23, 25, 53, 117, 118, 119,
 125, 126, 130, 131, 132, 133, 134, 135,
 139, 152, 162, 174, 175
global scale, 69
globalization, 139
google, 146
governance, 174
governments, 64
graffiti, 124
gravity, 166
Great Britain, ix, 63, 119, 125, 126, 131,
 132, 135, 139
Greece, 22, 99, 101, 104, 105, 118, 172
Greeks, 35, 101, 102
Greek-Turkish conflict, 25
growth, 88
Guantanamo, 40
guardian, 138, 152
guidance, 30, 138
Guinea, 16, 17, 41, 44, 45, 46

H

hair, 97
health, 122
height, 15, 31, 33, 51
hemisphere, 42
Hezbollah, 40
high school, 32, 106, 123, 172
higher education, 75, 90
highlands, 14, 41
Hillalian invasion, 14
history, ix, 16, 35, 36, 52, 55, 69, 75, 101,
 105, 108, 118, 123, 135, 142, 147, 168
Holy Books, 101
homes, 105, 114, 124, 133
homicide, 54
hospitality, 128
host, 118, 130
host societies, 119
hostage taking, 33

hostility, 95, 105, 128
house, 146, 158
housing, 96, 122, 129
human, 32, 37, 52, 84, 96, 135, 139
human nature, 139
human right, 32, 84, 96, 135
humanitarianism, 118
Hungary, 22, 110, 132
hybrid, 52, 107, 138

I

Iceland, 21
ideal, 75, 91, 114
ideals, 38, 126
identification, 88, 94, 113, 140
identity, 32, 35, 36, 38, 58, 62, 63, 70, 73,
 76, 79, 80, 83, 88, 94, 97, 102, 104, 113,
 115, 127, 134, 135, 138, 140, 149, 172
images, 109
imagination, 74
immigrants, 18, 23, 24, 118, 122, 127, 133,
 134, 174
immigration, 15, 23, 25, 119, 123, 125, 152
immunity, 50
imprisonment, 31, 55
impurities, 38, 91, 175
income, 111
independence, 23, 31, 32, 47, 49, 52, 54, 55,
 64, 73, 81, 82, 94, 95, 96, 102, 108, 110,
 112, 165, 169
India, 18, 19, 24, 62, 69, 125, 126
Indians, 69
individuals, 30, 39, 45, 95, 129, 138
Indonesia, 24, 117
industry, 62
ingredients, 106, 127
Ingush, 21, 93, 94, 96, 97, 171, 172
Ingushetia, 95
initiation, 138
instinct, 95
institutions, 47, 82, 107
integration, 119, 121, 126, 127, 132, 133
integrity, 32, 96
interference, 127

188 Index

intermediaries, 47, 61, 127
international terrorism, 105
intervention, 43, 90, 92, 114
invasions, 79, 129
Iran, 18, 80, 81, 82, 83, 84, 85, 114, 126, 129, 170
Iraq, 114, 129
Ireland, 20, 40, 125
iron, 19, 61, 69, 71
Iron Curtain, 131
Islam, ix, 13, 14, 15, 16, 17, 18, 21, 22, 24, 25, 26, 29, 32, 35, 36, 37, 38, 39, 42, 43, 44, 45, 47, 48, 51, 52, 53, 54, 55, 61, 62, 63, 64, 65, 66, 69, 70, 72, 73, 74, 75, 77, 79, 80, 81, 82, 83, 84, 87, 88, 89, 90, 91, 92, 93, 94, 96, 97, 99, 101, 102, 103, 104, 106, 107, 108, 109, 110, 111, 113, 117, 118, 123, 125, 126, 129, 134, 135, 137, 138, 139, 141, 142, 143, 144, 145, 146, 147, 148, 149, 150, 151, 152, 153, 154, 155, 156, 157, 158, 159, 160, 161, 162, 163, 164, 166, 167, 170, 172, 173, 175
Islamic law, 47, 55, 166, 169
Islamic movements, 166
Islamic society, 75, 106
Islamic state, 62, 63, 64, 85, 105, 167
Islamic world, 17, 19, 21, 39, 114
Islamism, 40, 81, 104, 142, 150
islands, 18, 71, 73, 75
isolation, 114, 122, 133
Israel, 84, 123
issues, 25, 32, 104, 105, 131, 135
Italy, 20, 24, 36, 63, 77, 101, 118
Ivory Coast, 16, 41, 42, 44, 45

J

Jamaica, 174
Jews, 85, 111, 123, 173
jihad, 33, 46, 52, 53, 57, 63, 88, 90, 126, 127, 134, 152, 167
jihadist, 66
jobless, 32
jumping, 13

just society, 91
justification, 90

K

Kenya, 18, 19, 62, 63, 66, 74, 169
kidnapping, 49, 95
kill, 135, 175
kinship, 17, 42, 62, 133
kinship network, 133
knees, 97
Kosovo, 22, 23, 25, 99, 101, 102, 103, 104, 107, 112, 114, 115, 118, 142, 160, 172
Kurds, 24, 118

L

labor shortage, 23, 24, 126
language skills, 133
languages, 48, 57
law enforcement, 121, 122, 174
laws, 19, 64
lead, 31, 81, 83, 165
leadership, 15, 32, 53, 75, 80, 84, 94
learning, 16, 17, 34, 38, 43, 44, 82, 93, 110, 133, 163, 164
Lebanon, 24, 40
legal protection, 132
liberation, 88
Liberia, 16, 18, 41
liberty, 89
Libya, vii, ix, 14, 15, 16, 29, 31, 34, 35, 36, 37, 38, 39, 40, 49, 50, 139, 140, 143, 155, 163, 165, 166
lifetime, 122
Lion, 37
literacy, 19, 70, 71
local community, 130
local conditions, 137
longevity, 137

M

Macedonia, 22, 23, 99, 102, 103, 105, 107, 112, 114, 142, 149, 173
magnet, 118
majority, 18, 20, 23, 48, 52, 62, 73, 74, 75, 87, 95, 104, 112, 117, 121, 128, 131, 169, 173
Malaysia, 108
man, 46, 65
manpower, 131
marginalization, 105, 134
marriage, 47, 64
Marx, 148, 159
Maryland, 150, 161, 177
mass, 23, 44, 96, 113
matter, 31, 35, 123
Mauritania, 15, 16, 17, 31, 34, 41, 44, 47, 49, 50
Mauritius, 18
meat, 62
media, 40, 114, 127
Mediterranean, 13, 20, 24, 29, 30, 61, 69, 111
melting, 127
membership, 24, 83, 84, 97, 105
mentor, 128
merchandise, 17
mergers, 143
Mesopotamia, 79
middle class, 32, 76, 121
Middle East, 13, 19, 21, 22, 23, 24, 41, 61, 62, 71, 73, 79, 84, 88, 89, 114, 123, 127, 147, 148, 155, 158, 159, 164
migrants, 24, 127, 131, 132
migration, 35, 56, 117, 118, 127, 133
militancy, 53, 65, 171
military, 14, 15, 16, 21, 22, 29, 30, 31, 32, 33, 42, 46, 49, 57, 66, 72, 87, 90, 94, 95, 96, 102, 110, 111, 112, 137, 139
militia, 96
militias, 39
Minneapolis, 158
minorities, 75, 105
mission, 26

mixing, 114
models, 175
moderates, 40, 107, 113, 171
modern science, 106
modern society, 26
modernization, 48, 64, 106, 123, 137, 139
Moldova, 22, 24
monopoly, 32
Montenegro, 22, 23, 24, 99, 107, 173
morality, 84
Morocco, 14, 15, 16, 20, 24, 29, 30, 31, 42, 44, 117, 164
mosaic, 30
Moscow, 90, 94, 96, 118, 149
Mozambique, 18, 61, 164
multiculturalism, 128, 130
multi-ethnic, 112
murder, 166
music, 46
Muslim, viii, ix, 14, 15, 16, 17, 18, 19, 20, 21, 22, 23, 24, 25, 26, 29, 30, 31, 32, 35, 36, 38, 39, 40, 41, 44, 46, 47, 48, 52, 53, 54, 55, 56, 57, 61, 62, 64, 70, 71, 72, 73, 74, 75, 76, 80, 81, 82, 84, 87, 88, 89, 91, 94, 95, 99, 103, 104, 106, 107, 109, 110, 113, 114, 115, 117, 118, 121, 122, 123, 124, 125, 126, 127, 128, 129, 130, 131, 132, 133, 135, 137, 138, 139, 141, 142, 143, 144, 145, 146, 148, 149, 150, 151, 152, 153, 155, 157, 159, 160, 161, 162, 163, 164, 165, 166, 167, 168, 169, 171, 172, 173, 174
Muslim diaspora, ix
Muslim extremists, 91, 123
Muslim states, 17, 20, 52
mutilation, 95

N

Nagorno-Karabakh, 24, 25, 80, 81, 84, 170
narcotics, 95
national character, 83
national community, 73
national identity, 35, 38, 80, 83, 102, 135, 140

National Party, 169
nationalism, 63, 73, 75, 81, 83, 102, 111, 125, 170
nationalists, 82, 111
nationality, 94
NATO, 23, 105, 114, 173
neglect, 75, 128
Netherlands, 21, 24, 117, 119
New Zealand, 127
Niger River, 46
Nigeria, vii, ix, 16, 17, 18, 41, 44, 45, 50, 51, 52, 53, 54, 55, 56, 57, 118, 139, 141, 143, 144, 145, 156, 167, 168
Nile, 13, 163
Nile River, 13
North Africa, vii, ix, 13, 14, 15, 16, 22, 23, 24, 27, 29, 30, 35, 37, 38, 41, 43, 46, 49, 61, 111, 114, 117, 137, 139, 141, 142, 153, 154, 163, 165
North America, 114
North Caucasus, 21, 87, 90, 92, 93, 96, 139, 148, 149, 159, 160, 171
Northern Ireland, 40
Norway, 24, 118
nuclear family, v

O

officials, 34, 54, 56, 92, 102, 106, 127, 174
oil, 18, 32, 33, 56, 57, 84, 85, 95, 104, 168
openness, 75
operations, 39, 90
opportunities, 127
oppression, 91
organ, 90, 169
organize, 33, 75, 174
Oromo, 18, 62
outreach, 91
overlay, 71
oxidation, 19

P

Pakistan, 24, 82, 114, 125, 126, 127, 128, 129, 174
Parliament, 128
participants, 69
partition, 113
patriotism, 75
peace, 30, 50, 54
peacekeeping, 50
penalties, 38, 90
permission, 64
perpetrators, 123
personal relations, 37
personal relationship, 37
Philadelphia, 147, 158
pipeline, 84
piracy, 36, 56, 57, 65, 168
platform, 66
playing, 23
pluralism, 34, 81
Poland, 111, 132
police, 57, 96, 130, 132
policy, 25, 47, 73, 75, 79, 84, 124, 127
political leaders, 94
political parties, 82, 103, 169
political power, 33, 174
political system, 85
politics, 29, 30, 83, 84
pollution, 126
popular support, 31
population, 18, 20, 22, 23, 24, 31, 36, 51, 52, 64, 72, 73, 76, 80, 82, 84, 87, 88, 89, 95, 97, 101, 103, 105, 106, 107, 110, 113, 117, 119, 121, 122, 125, 126, 127, 142, 147, 149, 151, 173
population pyramid, 23
porous borders, 49
Portugal, 20, 24, 118
poverty, 57, 108
prayer, 97
preferential treatment, 122
preservation, 123
presidency, 74, 115

Index 191

president, 33, 47, 66, 74, 82, 94, 95, 96, 111, 122, 167, 172
prestige, 38
primary school, 73
principles, 32, 114
privateers, 14, 30
programming, 97
propaganda, 82, 123
prosperity, 24, 56
protection, 110
protectorate, 74
public safety, 40
public schools, 174
publishing, 88
purity, 126

Q

qualifications, 133

R

race, 33
radicalism, 34, 83, 91, 107, 108, 114, 126, 129, 132, 134
radicalization, 129
radicals, 33, 44, 49, 83, 92, 107, 108, 128, 129, 134
radio, 48, 54
rainforest, 13, 14, 16, 18, 41, 44, 45, 163
Ramadan, 39, 82, 170
rape, 113
reality, 20, 30, 64, 104, 126
recession, 132
recognition, 85, 90
recruiting, 57, 114
Red Sea, 13, 18, 19, 41, 61, 69, 157, 163
reform, 17, 33, 42, 45, 75, 142, 146, 154, 158, 171
reformers, 48
refugees, 24, 25, 61, 84, 114, 118, 128, 150
regulations, 91, 138
relatives, 82, 93, 127
relief, 102

religion, ix, 13, 20, 21, 23, 31, 33, 35, 36, 39, 45, 54, 55, 63, 64, 67, 70, 72, 80, 81, 82, 83, 84, 88, 93, 108, 109, 113, 114, 115, 123, 124, 126, 132, 134, 138, 142, 164, 166, 170, 172
religiosity, 134
religious observances, 15
repair, 40
repression, 97
reputation, 50, 93, 128
requirements, 122
resentment, 63, 107
resettlement, 118
resilience, 139
resistance, 25, 31, 37, 38, 47, 63, 88, 93, 94, 101, 102, 137, 165, 166, 171
resources, 84, 107, 108, 112, 143
response, 72, 89, 102, 108, 139
restaurants, 133
restrictions, 110
retaliation, 56
retirement, 122
rhetoric, 126, 127
rights, 32, 75, 84, 96, 110, 132, 135
Romania, 22, 132
root, 38, 107, 108, 137, 139
routes, 13, 16, 51, 53, 72, 164
rubber, 33
rules, 91, 94, 135
rural areas, 17, 30, 53, 55, 89, 90, 101, 108
Russia, 21, 22, 25, 77, 82, 84, 88, 90, 94, 95, 96, 117, 118, 142, 148, 159
Rwanda, 18

S

safety, 40
Salvation Army, 32, 33
sanctuaries, 50
Sarajevo, 173
Sarkozy, Nicolas, 122
Saudi Arabia, 18, 48, 65, 82, 83, 84, 104, 105, 106, 107, 121, 126
Scandinavia, 21
scholarship, 74

school, 19, 25, 30, 32, 45, 46, 47, 48, 53, 54, 57, 65, 69, 70, 73, 74, 75, 88, 89, 93, 95, 96, 97, 104, 106, 122, 123, 129, 133, 169, 171, 172, 174
science, 48, 172
scripts, 69, 111
second generation, 122, 133
second language, 19, 52
secondary education, 75
sectarianism, 76
secularism, 85, 123, 126
security, 53, 96, 122, 127, 128, 138, 143, 174
segregation, 97, 130
seizure, 36
self-consciousness, 111
self-interest, 47
self-regulation, 128
September 11, 39, 104
Serbia, 22, 24, 99, 103, 107, 109, 111, 112, 113, 172, 173
Serbs, 23, 103, 111, 112, 113, 114, 173
services, 47, 97, 109, 121, 130, 133
settlements, 18, 29, 35, 45, 62
sex, 33, 91, 129
Sharia, 16, 25, 32, 37, 38, 39, 40, 51, 54, 55, 56, 64, 84, 88, 89, 91, 94, 95, 101, 115, 127, 130, 145, 148, 156, 159, 166
Shiites, 83
shores, 128, 168
shortage, 126
Siberia, 94
Sierra Leone, 16, 18, 41
silk, 19, 71
silver, 16, 42
Sinai, 13
slavery, 54, 72
slaves, 17, 38, 42, 53, 72, 164
social development, 74
social life, 82
social network, 133
social order, 74
social reality, 126
social structure, 88
social welfare, 40

society, ix, 25, 26, 48, 52, 54, 55, 65, 66, 75, 91, 93, 94, 106, 110, 111, 118, 124, 133, 137, 139, 140
sociology, ix
solution, 112
Somali coast, 14
Somalia, vii, ix, 18, 57, 61, 62, 63, 64, 65, 66, 67, 118, 139, 145, 146, 157, 164, 168, 169
South America, 16
South Asia, 23, 75, 117, 129, 152, 161, 169
South Ossetia, 24, 25, 82
Southeast Asia, 61, 89, 114
Southern Caucasus, 77
sovereignty, 30, 35
Soviet Union, 21, 25, 65, 80, 89, 94, 114, 117, 118, 132, 148, 159, 160
Spain, 20, 24, 47, 111, 118, 153, 163, 164
stability, 139
standard of living, 110
stars, 66
state, ix, 16, 17, 18, 19, 20, 22, 26, 29, 32, 33, 36, 38, 41, 43, 45, 46, 47, 48, 49, 50, 51, 52, 53, 54, 56, 57, 61, 62, 63, 64, 65, 71, 80, 81, 82, 84, 85, 95, 102, 103, 104, 105, 110, 112, 115, 126, 129, 130, 132, 135, 164, 165, 166, 167, 168, 169, 170, 173, 174
state control, 33
statistics, 55, 117
stress, 16, 37, 57, 81, 88, 106, 107
strictures, 38, 91, 97
structure, 18, 88, 93, 119, 138
style, 70
succession, 33
Sudan, 13, 15, 16, 17, 41, 46, 51, 58, 61, 105, 141, 144, 145, 153, 155, 156, 163
suicide, 128
suicide bombers, 128
suppression, 65, 81, 94
surveillance, 104
survival, 81, 137
Swahili, 18, 19, 69, 70, 71, 73, 139, 141, 145, 146, 153, 154, 157, 164, 168, 169
Sweden, 24, 25, 118

Index

Switzerland, 20, 24, 118, 119
Syria, 15, 24, 103, 112

T

tactics, 91
takeover, 44, 111
talent, 31
Taliban, 114, 134
tanks, 96
Tanzania, vii, 18, 19, 69, 71, 73, 74, 76, 139, 146, 157, 158, 169
target, 52
taxation, 52
taxes, 53
teachers, 37, 45, 48, 52, 73
telecommunications, 54
tension, 65, 74, 83
tenure, 110
territorial, 102
territory, 46, 51, 65, 72, 90, 113, 114, 124, 132, 173
terrorism, 90, 91, 92, 95, 96, 105, 106, 121, 128, 134, 143, 171
terrorist activities, 165
terrorist acts, 33, 114, 118, 128
terrorist attack, 39, 76
terrorist groups, 34, 127, 129, 174
terrorist organization, 65, 134
terrorists, 104, 129, 132
textbooks, 74
textiles, 19, 71
Third World, 157
threats, 76, 124, 128
tobacco, 46
Togo, 16, 18, 41, 45
trade, 13, 14, 16, 17, 36, 37, 41, 42, 43, 49, 51, 61, 62, 71, 72, 110, 139, 164, 167
traditional authorities, 127
traditional practices, 138
traditions, 37, 57, 76, 114, 137
training, 66, 89, 95, 107, 114, 129, 134, 174
traits, 139
transactions, 70
transformation, 47, 95

transmission, 13, 38, 41, 163
transportation, 54, 96, 122
treatment, 111, 122, 129, 137
Turkey, 18, 22, 25, 30, 36, 80, 81, 82, 85, 88, 103, 105, 106, 131, 132, 134, 170
Turkmenistan, 80
Turks, 21, 22, 102, 105, 114, 118, 132, 133, 134, 135, 158, 166

U

Ukraine, 21, 111
unemployment rate, 115, 133
unhappiness, 50
unions, 24
united, viii, ix, 24, 25, 38, 39, 66, 112, 117, 118, 125, 128, 129, 134, 152, 162, 174
United Kingdom (UK), viii, ix, 24, 25, 117, 125, 129, 152, 162, 174
United Nations, 38, 66, 104, 128, 174
United States, 25, 39, 112, 118, 129, 134, 152, 162
universities, 90, 91, 106, 108, 113, 123
urban, 25, 32, 44, 49, 53, 55, 65, 73, 94, 97, 101, 110, 114, 121, 122, 127, 132, 174
urban areas, 25, 44, 53, 65, 101, 114, 122, 132, 174
urban population, 73
USSR, 89, 159
Uzbekistan, 134, 174

V

vacuum, 105
veneration, 30, 37, 52, 138
videos, 134
violence, 25, 33, 48, 55, 56, 82, 92, 96, 118, 124, 128
volunteers, 114
vote, 33, 39, 104
vulnerability, 125

W

wages, 127
Wahhabism, 90, 91, 126
Wales, 125
war, 14, 23, 33, 36, 55, 63, 106, 111, 112,
  113, 114, 118, 134, 145, 150, 151, 162,
  168, 173
warlords, 66, 95
Washington, 146, 150, 151, 157
water, 36, 95
Waziristan, 134
wealth, 16, 34, 41, 44, 51, 53, 62, 71, 84,
  95, 163, 164
weapons, 70, 95
wear, 70, 97, 123, 130
websites, 40
welfare, 40
West Africa, vii, ix, 13, 16, 17, 18, 24, 34,
  41, 43, 45, 46, 47, 51, 52, 117, 123, 129,
  137, 139, 141, 143, 144, 145, 153, 155,
  156, 163, 164, 165, 166, 167, 174

West Indies, 127
western education, 32
Western Europe, 23, 25, 117, 118, 139
wholesale, 111, 173
wood, 69
workers, 24, 95, 122, 131, 132
World Health Organization, 122
World War I, 126

Y

Yemen, 71, 105, 106, 128
young people, 25, 33, 74, 91, 122, 126, 134
Yugoslavia, 103, 111, 112, 114, 133, 150,
  161

Z

Zimbabwe, 61, 71